Mara
PJ

by

Tim Ryan

BLACKWATER PRESS

Printed in Ireland at the press of the publishers

© Blackwater Press 1992
8 Airton Road,
Tallaght,
Dublin 24.

ISBN 0 86121 406 4 (HBK)
ISBN 0 86121 490 0 (PBK)

Editor
Anna O'Donovan

Design & Layout
Anne Lewis

Front Cover
Colman Doyle

TO THE MEMORY OF MY PARENTS

Tim Ryan is a political reporter with the *Irish Press*. He is the co-author of *Ballinspittle: Moving Statues and Faith* (Mercier 1985) with UCC psychologist Dr Jurek Kirakowski.

Contents

Foreword

The 12 months before April 1992 had been traumatic.

That period had witnessed, among other developments, the disintegration of the Soviet Union, and the break-up of Yugoslavia.

At home the Irish rugby squad had taken a hammering. And the other major watershed of the year had been the departure from high office of Charles Haughey after 12 years as Taoiseach of the land.

But for one man, time appeared to have stood still.

In April 1991 PJ Mara had attended the prestigious IMI Conference in Killarney in the company of the Taoiseach, Charles Haughey, the principal guest speaker. Drawing on his superb social skills, Mara had mingled with business people and journalists alike, doing the same thing as he had for the previous 21 years, carefully moulding Haughey's public image.

Twelve months later, in April 1992, there was PJ Mara again at the IMI Conference, again cruising close to the real seat of power. This time he was accompanying GPA chief Tony Ryan, the principal guest speaker.

At 50 years of age, PJ Mara's career has been spectacular by any comparison. Born into a lower middle-class Dublin family in 1942, his father had died when he was just seven years old, leaving his mother to rear two young children alone.

The visit of President John F Kennedy to Ireland in 1963 helped to inspire the young Drumcondra man into taking an active role in politics, a role that was to put him into contact with one of the most controversial politicians of all time, Charles Haughey.

His years with him, initially very much on the outside in the wake of the Arms Trial and later as Government Press Secretary, give a fascinating insight into both the workings of the Fianna Fail party machine and the operation of Government.

Mara's fascination with Haughey is a story in itself. Attracted by the twin prospects of gaining and using power, and using his own political skills, Mara professed a unique loyalty to his Boss in a way that had never been seen before in Irish public life.

He played a central role in the second coming of Charles Haughey, ignominiously sacked from the Cabinet by Jack Lynch in 1970, only to reappear as Taoiseach nine years later.

Government Press Secretaries there certainly had been, but they had come to do a professional job and duly departed upon the fall of the Government. But PJ Mara brought an entirely new dimension to the job. Viewed largely as the Taoiseach's personal spokesman, rather than that of the Government, Mara weaved a web of political fascination around the corridors of Leinster House.

The possessor of superb social skills and a gregarious open manner, Mara, who while taking his work seriously, liked to meet journalists, editors and politicians, and others with whom he had to do business in a social atmosphere, particularly in the pubs and restaurants around Government Buildings and Leinster House. Sitting aloft on a high stool in the Horse Shoe bar – smoking a Monte Cristo cigar, PJ claims he liked the cut and thrust of this kind of exchange of anecdotes, slander, calumny, all of it generally unfit to print.

'Too many people, who should really know better take themselves too seriously,' says Mara. 'They are usually alone in so doing. Anyway I have always believed in the truth of the old saying: "Humour is the hallmark of high intelligence!"'

When he finally left his post as Government Press Secretary in April 1992, his successor, former RTE presenter Sean Duginan asked him if he intended to write a book.

'No,' replied Mara, 'I still want to live in this town!'

PJ Mara would find it difficult to write a book. As a man who even found it difficult to write a letter, he lived by the telephone. The material evidence of his years in Government Buildings is sparse.

Any future student of politics hoping to publish the edited works of PJ Mara will have a very slim volume indeed! Apart from love notes left for his wife Breda in the early hours of the morning, and a few dozen official letters, there is little other written evidence of his period in office.

Yet, when the history of the 1970s and '80s will be written about, PJ Mara will be a very definite character. Although first and foremost loyal to Charles Haughey, his personality refused to be confined to a secondary role.

But it was the arrival of the satirical radio series, *Scrap Saturday*, which made Mara a national figure. Each Saturday morning for half an hour, comic Dermot Morgan and his team brought the nation to its knees with caricatures of a greedy, avaricious Taoiseach and his bungling Press Secretary, 'Maaara'.

The following pages are an attempt to tell the story of how a young Drumcondra lad became friendly with a senior politician who had fallen from grace, and how in a most extraordinary way, they set about the very serious business of regaining power.

They succeeded where others failed, and their continued teamwork in Government reflected the knowledge and experience they had learned in those hard years of the 1970s.

Much of the happenings will forever remain a secret. Some events are best left untold, and others cannot be told because of the laws of libel and defamation!

But the life and times of Patrick James Mara, as we know them, make him one of the most remarkable Dublin figures of this century.

Acknowledgements

In writing a book of this kind, a number of interviews had to be conducted on the basis that I would not name my sources. My sincere thanks to them.

I would like also to especially thank PJ Mara for agreeing to a number of interviews, especially the one which forms the basis for the book's final chapter 'Reflections'. Without his co-operation, this book would not have been possible. My sincere appreciation to his wife, Breda, son John and sister Marian for their patience.

Thanks also to the library and photographic department of the *Irish Press*, Dermot Morgan and Cue Productions, the staff of the Oireachtas Library and Dublin Corporation archives.

To the many people that agreed to be interviewed about PJ Mara I am ever grateful. Their names appear throughout the book.

I owe a special word of thanks to Niamh O'Connor of the Fianna Fail Press Office, TP O'Mahony of the *Cork Examiner*, Michael O'Sullivan of RTE, Hugh Lambert and John Garvey of the *Irish Press* for their constant encouragement and good humour.

A very special thanks to John Cooney who read the manuscript and offered helpful suggestions.

Finally my special thanks to editor, Anna O'Donovan and to John O'Connor of Blackwater Press for bringing it all together.

1

Pin-Striped Short Pants

'I tended to talk my way out of situations, to avoid confrontations.
There were too many hardy boys around and in those days you could
get the shit kicked out of you very easily!'

Few things can excite young boys like trains. The sound and power of
these great inventions fascinates the minds and totally absorbs inquisi-
tive young lads. An ideal viewing point is from overhead, preferably
from a bridge.

A mile to the west of Drumcondra, at Claude Road, where the
Sligo railway line crosses the main Belfast road, is such a point. The
bridge, crafted in the Hammond Lane Foundry, has not changed
since it was first erected. From it you get an ideal view of the
approaching passenger and goods trains as they leave Dublin's
Connolly station on their journey west.

It was here in the late 1940s that Garda John Mara would bring his
young son, PJ, in the evenings when he had finished work.

Having returned to his home at nearby 40 Millmount Avenue, he
would take his son to either Iona Road church or his own parish
church, Corpus Christi, where he would kneel and pray for a while.
Then he would walk the quarter of a mile or so down the narrow red-
bricked streets of Drumcondra to the viaduct. There the two would
stand, father and son, and watch the passing trains with total interest.

Wherever Garda John Mara went in the evenings, he brought his
young son with him.

'I remember him making breakfast in the kitchen on a Sunday
morning,' PJ recalls. 'Going for walks to see the trains passing at

Claude Road in Drumcondra where there's a pedestrian bridge we would watch the trains come up and choo-choo…that sort of thing.'

A kind-hearted man, it was to him the young PJ turned on his first morning at the local St Pat's National School.

'I want to go back to say Goodbye to my Mammy!' he screamed repeatedly at his father. His Dad brought him back home again, but there was little comfort to be got from Mrs Mara who had no patience with this sort of carry-on. PJ was quickly and firmly installed in the front row in Babies!

John Mara was born in 1908 into a strong Cumann Na nGael family in Clonard, Co. Meath. The young Clonard man joined the fledgling Free State police in the 1920s. He first served in Castledermot before being transferred to the little village of Myshall in Co. Carlow.

While stationed there, he met a young girl from the banks of the Corrib, Sabina O'Sullivan, who was minding children for a local family. The two fell in love and got married. Shortly afterwards Garda Mara was transferred to Dublin and bought a house in Millmount Ave., close to Drumcondra village.

Their son, Patrick James, was born on March 13, 1942 – sharing his birthday with the notorious Nazi doctor, Joseph Mengele. Millmount Avenue was a natural lower middle-class area to choose as there were already five or six garda families living in the vicinity. A famous Garda Superintendent, Micky Gill, then Head of the Special Branch, lived on nearby Walsh Road.

Gill was one of the so-called Broy Harriers, recruited by Col. Eamon Broy on the instructions of Eamon De Valera. A former assistant in Clery's on O'Connell St., his first rank was that of Detective Sergeant. He proved very capable in rooting out the IRA squads and quickly rose through the ranks to become Chief Superintendent.

It was unusual for such a high-ranking officer to live in a Corporation house, and he was given full-time security when the Government executed IRA rebels in the 1940s.

Garda John Mara was one of the last members of the force to do duty inside the GPO. Not a lover of point duty, his main interest was in helping out pensioners who were unable to write. His compassion for the elderly went beyond his job, and his daughter Marian recalls him frequently leaving his sick bed to sign forms so that poor people could collect their benefits on time.

In February 1949 he had become ill with what appeared to be a very bad ulcer. When he finally went to the Garda doctor he was simply given tablets and told to go home. Many guards would frequently slip over to the doctor to get a sick certificate signed in order to get a few days off to take care of their vegetable allotments, so Garda John Mara's absence alerted no particular interest.

During Christmas his sickness worsened, and he died in February, 1950 from cancer in Harold's Cross Hospice for the Dying. He was aged 42. Making ends meet for a young family in post-war Dublin was difficult, even with a breadwinner in the family. Without one, it was sheer hell.

Yet this was the reality that faced Sabina Mara in the cold February of 1950. She had buried her late husband on a Friday morning, and the following Monday a Superintendent arrived to collect John's uniform. Sympathising with her plight, the Superintendent strongly advised Mrs Mara to return home to 'her people in the country'.

The comment infuriated her, and she became more determined than ever to raise her family on her own.

Sabina O'Sullivan had been born into strong Republican stock on the banks of the Corrib. The daughter of a small farmer she went to work as a child-minder for friends of the family in Myshall, Co. Carlow where she met her husband.

Strong Civil War traditions led to tension in the home at election time. 'My father would always say to my mother to be sure and vote for the Fine Gael candidate, but she would promptly dash off and vote for De Valera!' recalls Marian.

Number 40 Millmount Road, Drumcondra is a small two-bed-roomed town house. There Sabina Mara looked after her two children, PJ and Marian, on the miserly pension amounting to £1 per week.

Her health had not been great and she had spent many years in hospital as a small child. She received her First Holy Communion in hospital while recovering from a major knee operation, which left her with a permanent limp.

To supplement her income, Sabina Mara took in two girls as boarders until her own family needed the room. She bought a knitting machine, and trained herself in how to use it.

Her daily routine began at 6am when she cleaned the house and got breakfast ready for PJ and Marian at 8. Having seen them off to school, she would have the back or side of a jumper knitted up before going to daily Mass at 10am. Then it was back to her machine until lunch-time when the children came in for an hour's break.

The afternoon saw her return to work, only to break for tea at 6pm. She never saw bed before 12 midnight. Friday broke her routine. On that day Sabina Mara cleaned the house from top to bottom before the children came home from school.

From the day her husband died until PJ and Marian were grown up and able to look after themselves, Mrs Mara never went outside the door to any sort of entertainment. 'She didn't believe in it, nor could she afford it,' says Marian. 'We had a good fire, plenty to eat, and a place to lie down. She was a very good manager.'

Later in life when people spoke of the country being in bad debt, Sabina would lose her patience and declare: 'They don't know how to manage money, what they need is a good lesson in housekeeping!'

Life was simple and straight-forward for a young Dublin lad like PJ Mara. Too young to have any real memories of his father, he quickly began to make the best use of his environment. He loved to go out and play with his mates, notably Michael Harnett, later Director of Elections for Charles Haughey.

Together they would kick a can around, or play 'Combo', a game where they chalked in goalposts on a gable-end and tried to score. Or they would go to nearby Griffith Park which had a disputed piece of land at the end. This 'jungle' was a kid's paradise, where all sorts of imaginary battles were fought.

They used to hang around in gangs, get up on boxes to make speeches and see who could talk the longest.

But PJ also liked to play with the bigger lads. He tried to follow his father's philosophy that you should always mix with people that knew a little more than yourself. And he mimicked everybody and everything.

When the gas man came, PJ went around after him and read all the meters. He read the ESB meters. A man used to come round from the Corporation and test the water for leaks. PJ would do the same thing. He would get a stick, go to doors and say to women: 'I'm sorry, but you'll have to do something about your water!' The sharp-witted Mara was already emerging.

But he was careful to protect himself. 'I tended to talk my way out of situations, to avoid confrontations. There were too many hardy boys around and in those days and you could get the shit kicked out of you very easily!'

Number 40 Millmount Avenue backed onto the old Lemon's sweet factory, now the site of a luxury town house development. Discarded waste chocolate was manna from Heaven for the young PJ and his mates as they raced to the bins to steal it before the security man had a chance to catch them!

Everybody calling to the Mara home entered via the back lane. Anybody who knocked at the front door was a stranger. Already popular within the area, evening time would see a steady flow of youngsters to Number 40 with the same question: 'Is PJ in?'

Eamon Dunphy, then a lad in short trousers, lived on nearby Richmond Road, across the road from Tolka Park.

'Eamon says that I never did anything really interesting or significant when we were growing up,' says PJ. 'He says I was a bit boring and wore pin-striped short trousers. And he has this memory of me that I always looked like I was going to a meeting, but I think Eamon's memory is playing tricks on him.

'There was a very nice mixture of people,' Eamon recalls, 'and there were lots of characters of whom, in his own way, PJ was one of the most prominent. But the area was uniquely cosmopolitan.'

Eamon was five years younger than PJ.

'PJ was always going somewhere, either going to a meeting or coming back. He was always very smartly dressed and stood a bit apart from everyone else. There were some very hard cases around the area too, along with some brilliant people.'

Dunphy was the noted footballer and spent most of his time playing football. Other footballers in the area were Tommy Emerson who played for Drums and Frank O'Neill from nearby Ballybough who played for Arsenal and Ireland.

'PJ was never a sporty type,' says Dunphy. 'He was suave and very sophisticated, but he would always stop and gossip and was aware of street life. I always felt he was keeping files on us all, potential voters for the future!'

Football, soccer, the library, and when they were older, dances in Glasnevin and the CYMS in Fairview, were the simple leisure activities of the day.

Neither PJ nor Eamon Dunphy, nor anyone else paid any heed to the GAA ban on 'foreign' games.

'We never made any distinction between soccer, hurling and Gaelic football,' says Eamon. 'The two big teams were the Drums soccer squad and the Dublin Football team.

They would often go along to Croke Park mid-week to watch hurling teams like St Vincent's take on teams like Glen Rovers from the heart of Cork city.

The folk heroes of the time were players like Kit Lawlor of Drums, a beautiful footballer, who later played for Doncaster Rovers and the Irish team, Pa Daly and, in later years Alan Kelly and Bunny Fullam.

There were songs too, to commemorate great football teams, like the one about the 1955 Dublin Football team (to the tune of McNamara's band):

'My name is Dano Mahony, I'm the captain of the Blues,
We're nearly all from Vincent's and we very seldom lose,
O'Leary, Boyle and Heffernan will give you all a thrill,
The way they throw the ball around, and score goals at will.'

The 1963 team which defeated Galway in the All-Ireland also had a song which began:

'O'Leary and Foley, and Flynn as a goalie,
The blue and white colours we'll wave in victory...'

'Just knocking around. Going to the Drum Cinema. You rarely went into town – it just didn't arise. If you did, it was kind of adventure, a real break.'

Later the Teddy Boy era arrived and PJ's now famous interest in style first manifested itself. 'These guys from our neighbourhood went off to England looking quite ordinary. But they came home at Christmas with all this exotic gear: drape jackets, drainpipe trousers, the soapy crepe-sole shoes and duck's arse haircuts. I loved that whole thing. I don't think I had the duck's arse haircut. No, I was always losing my hair.'

But the Maras enjoyed one luxury that few other children had access to. Every summer, once school had ended they packed their bags and headed for long holidays on the farm of one of Sabina's brothers in Oughterard. The schools would close on a Friday and the Maras would be heading west on Monday morning. They would not return until three or four days before the reopening. There PJ and

Marian added a rural dimension to their lives. 'I learned how to milk a cow, how to feed calves and hens, cut turf on the bog, and save the hay. We had the best of both worlds. These days young people are being brought out and shown model farms as a kind of holiday event, whereas we had the real thing.'

Oughterard was a lovely spot in the summer. The view out across the Corrib looking over to Cong was magnificent. Life in the West was slow and easy.

This summer break for the Maras aroused curiosity among his Drumcondra mates.

'It was a source of awe for the rest of us,' recalls Michael Harnett. 'It made him a little different, a little unusual. We used to think of the West as in the films. This fellow would say "Goodbye" and head off to some mythical place. It seemed romantic and different.'

School for PJ was St Pat's where he attended the old Number One school, where everything was taught through Irish, ·and he later attended Colaiste Mhuire in Parnell Square.

'You either went to the tech. or the secondary school. If you wanted to go to secondary school you could go either to the Christian Brothers in O'Connell's or the North Circular Road, St Vincent's in Glasnevin or Colaiste Mhuire in Parnell Square. But if your family had money, you could go to Belvedere College. I went to Colaiste Mhuire.'

At school he immersed himself in hurling and football.

'I was reasonably good at games and would always get on the school team. But I would never be remembered five years later for winning goals or last-gasp points from 70 yards.'

The games left their mark on PJ, literally. Today, he still bears a scar on the side of his mouth, acquired while playing hurling at St Pat's. The clatter of an opponent's hurley split his mouth.

'Soaked in blood on the way home I could put my finger through my cheek. My old lady freaked and gave me a good belt. It's a commentary on the social services of the time – you're pumping blood and all you got was a good thump!'

But help was at hand. Next door neighbours, the Cunninghams had no children of their own, but were besotted with PJ. As soon as he saw the gash Mick Cunningham rushed in through the back garden – almost decapitating himself on Mrs Mara's washing line – grabbed PJ and took him on the bar of his bicycle down to Temple St hospital. PJ was admitted and stitched together.

A clever, but undistinguished scholar, PJ Mara enjoyed learning. History lessons, like those on Mussolini – *uno duce, una voce* – would remain with him, only to re-appear many years later in the political correspondents' room in Leinster House.

'I wasn't a particularly distinguished student at school. I got four honours in my Inter Cert and three in my Leaving. I would be a perfect example of hope for undistinguished students. There is life and hope after a mediocre performance at school!'

Today, PJ Mara is fulsome in his praise for the Christian Brothers.

'I despise those people – many of them contemporaries of mine – who try to run them down, or disparage the education they received from the Brothers.

'Generations of boys from my class and background owe their careers and education to those men and they should be more generous and grateful and acknowledge that now.

'To men like Brother Lee, Brother Garvey, Brother McGrath and Brother Feeney, who were in Colaiste Mhuire at that time, I owe an enormous debt of gratitude.'

2

A Very Distinguished Messenger Boy

'To be good at anything, you've got to be devoted to it; you've got to give it your total undivided, unremitting application.'

PJ Mara was always a man in a hurry.

'He was quiet in the house and read a lot,' recalls Marian. 'But sometimes when you talked to him, he would not even be listening. A lot of his mother's business attitudes passed onto him, almost without him noticing. She felt strongly about things, and consequently it rubbed off on him.'

Always a reader, from his early days he wore a beaten path to Drumcondra library which was around the corner from his home. Now the owner of an impressive library at his Wellington Road home, even in the late 1950s he began to put together his first collection of Penguin paperbacks.

His mother had hoped her son would get a secure, permanent job in the bank or the Civil Service. But even in those days, the exams were highly competitive.

However, PJ was not interested in a 'boring' career, and already the spirit of private enterprise was budding.

During the year of his Leaving Cert his mother packed him off to sit the Junior Executive exam in the Civil Service. PJ went the first day, but decided enough was enough – he mitched the second.

The weeks passed and no results came. Finally Sabina Mara rang a cousin in the Civil Service who quickly explained why PJ was not being called to work.

The young Mara was then subjected to the full wrath of his mother. Not a word was spoken for weeks! In the Mara house there was one rule – you did not try to deceive people!

But his first taste of real work and earning his own money had come a few years earlier. Joe Connolly owned a greengrocer's shop in Dorset Street from which he supplied all the hospitals, hotels and nursing homes in the locality. One summer Joe hired PJ – and his bike – for £1.12 ½p a week.

The first task of the day was to go to the fruit market with Joe Connolly to buy the goods, and then to put the orders together.

'I used to go and deliver fruit and vegetables to the back doors of convents and hotels. Looking back it was total f*** savagery. I used to start at seven in the morning and not finish until after six in the evening. There was a half day on Thursday – from 2pm – but you worked your butt off all day on Saturday.'

'When it came to pay time, there was an old bollox of a clerk who would sit in the back of the shop and would say: "Now what age are you, sonny? I see you are entitled, under Labour Court regulations, to one pound, two shillings and six pence." It used to become a big ceremony handing this over in an envelope... and I was providing my own bike! I was the most potentially distinguished messenger boy in the north city at that time.'

'The only compensation was in chatting up the young ones who worked in the hotels. Sometimes you got to deliver to hotel reception, and there were some smashing looking receptionists with beautifully polished fingernails. I often fancied my chances. But no! I was the delivery boy, no matter how potentially distinguished!'

His first job, after leaving school, was in Boland's Mills. A Mr O'Connor who was friendly with the Christian Brothers used to fix fellows up with jobs there.

PJ's task was physical, and dirty. It involved taking in the grain, checking it, taking samples for bushel weight and moisture content. The pay was £3.50 per week.

In the meantime his mother and sister, Marian, had gone to Oughterard for their summer holidays. One morning a letter arrived at Oughterard from PJ stating that he was choking from the dust at Boland's. It wasn't exactly what he had in mind as a career.

But, again, there was little sympathy from Sabina Mara. She wrote back:

'Dear PJ, If I spent my money on fees in Colaiste Mhuire to have you choked with dust in Boland's Mills, then go right ahead and do that! Mother.'

In his next letter PJ informed his mum that he had got an interview with the accountant and was now employed in the office, and earning more money!

The quest to improve his position in life was endless. Daily, PJ would answer job advertisements. If a job offered £1 more than you were earning, you applied for it.

His second job was to be crucial to his future business career. It was at Allied Textiles in Chapelizod. There he worked in the cost office where garments were designed and planned.

'They had a work study team there, with whom I worked closely. It was an interesting time and I learned a lot from it. I think I always had a yearning for the textile industry.'

PJ's next move was to Thom Spruyt Ltd, a small packaging company, part of the Hely Group, later taken over by Smurfits. There he learned the art of packaging before moving on to Gallahers, the cigarette company, as a management trainee in Belfast. The company was planning to open a factory in Tallaght and PJ stayed with them for a short time.

By now he had built up a series of contacts in the textile industry. His newly-wed spouse, Breda, who worked part-time as a model, was also interested in fashion. The lure of the rag trade was inescapable.

Through two business contacts, Willie Murray and Ronnie Murphy, PJ organised a small premises in Dorset St, and started a small clothing company, Beeline, aptly named after his wife. The company specialised in children's clothing for the chain stores and sold them mainly to Penneys and Dunnes.

The business thrived. Expansion meant a new premises and Beeline moved to a bright new plant in the Hay Market, near Irish Distillers. By now PJ and Breda were employing fifty people. Along came Penneys and bought him out. PJ was glad, prospects were not good, the market was being filled with goods from south-east Asia. When all the creditors were paid, the Maras ended up with a tidy profit of £30,000, a lot of money in the pre-oil rise days of the early 1970s.

The Maras' next venture was not as successful, in fact it was a disaster. By 'a series of accidents' PJ Mara found himself in the furniture, carpets and floor covering business. At first he operated from the Hay Market and later from Moss St. Contracts for jobs were secured through architects and others. But there were a lot of 'rogues' in the business as well.

PJ Mara is reluctant, still, to talk about this business. It has left a blank, and he doesn't want to think about it.

'It turned out to be pretty awful. There were people owed money. It was just a f*** disaster. We must have been nuts! Part of my problem was that I was so preoccupied with politics, I had no real commitment to what I was doing day by day. My mind was on other things. We were making a living out of it, but it was always a struggle.

'You were always rushing to make a lodgement and rushing to make sure you made your payments. It just wasn't a life. It wasn't the sort of business you could make any real money in. It was too easy to get into. You had all kinds of people doing it. It was going the same way as the clothing business, only we had got out of that in time.'

PJ Mara had reached the end of his business career, for the time being at least.

Looking back as a businessman, he says he was 'mediocre'. 'To be good at anything , you've got to be devoted to it; you've got to give it your total, undivided, unremitting application, which is what I did with the Government Press Secretary job. The whole thing with me, I think, is that I was always deflected by politics. Even when I was in business my mind wasn't fully there – it was doing other things.'

The political bug had taken root.

3

Rocking Chair Politics

'I took a very strong view that Haughey had been very harshly treated for all kinds of reasons. I still think, to this day, that he was wrongly dismissed. Other people agreed to something for which they would not later take responsibility.'

President John F Kennedy's election as President of the United States in 1960 gave new hope across Europe. Nowhere was it more welcomed than in Ireland where Sean Lemass' Government was finally beginning to get things moving.

The news that he would visit Ireland in the summer of 1963 created a new buzz in Irish political life. Everyone loved the emigrant's son, and his picture hung beside Pope John XXIII and the Sacred Heart in many Irish homes.

The enthusiasm surrounding the visit had not missed the youthful inhabitants of Dublin's Millmount Avenue. The new President fired the imaginations of school friends PJ Mara and Michael Harnett.

PJ could hardly contain himself at the news of the President's arrival. The fact that Kennedy would be driving in from Dublin Airport meant that he would almost be passing by their home, right over Tolka bridge in Drumcondra.

On the morning of the visit PJ was up at dawn. After breakfast he took his mother's rocking chair and carried it the quarter of a mile to Tolka bridge. There he sat with Michael Harnett and other friends until the President passed by. They waved and screamed as the motorcade drove by, like the thousands of others packed along the route.

Like the rest, the visit affected the young Dublin lads, boosting their sense of a new Ireland.

'We did have a sense of the Republic,' recalls Michael Harnett.'We were also convinced that there should be a united Ireland. After all, we were Christian Brothers' lads, and you can't underestimate that, even though it does get overlaid with other things down the years.'

But curiously Pope John XXIII did not figure among PJ's heroes because he found the switch from the eternal beauty of the Latin mass to the English vernacular mundane and unsettling.

As an alter-boy in the Jesuit Chruch of St Francis Xavier in Gardiner St in the north Dublin inner city, he had learned to love the rhythm of the Latin language.

'Intribo ad altra Dei,' the priest would recite at 6am Mass each morning.

'Ad Deum, qui laetificat juventutem meum,' the young PJ would respond enthusiastically.

Young PJ's enthusiasm was also displayed on the soccer field where he imitated the dazzling, dribbling skills of Glasgow Celtic's Charlie Tully, one of the great soccer stars of the 1950s, a Belfast Protestant who played for Celtic. Another great hero of PJ's from that Celtic team, who won the League Cup Final in Hampden Park in 1954 was Jock Stein, afterwards a legendery manager of Glasgow Celtic and Scotland.

PJ Mara might never have joined Fianna Fail, had his father lived. But his mother, Sabina, unconsciously reinforced the Republican tradition in her son.

He first joined the party in 1963 – the year of the Kennedy visit – when he was 21 years old.

'I had a friend, Michael Murphy, whose father was a very strong member of Fianna Fail. His father used to insist that Michael should go to the Cumann meeting, at 72 Amiens St, the party constituency headquarters. Also, at that time we used to go to a dance in Mount Pleasant Tennis Club. Rather than wait around for Michael, I used to go into the Cumann meeting. So that's how I joined the O'Donovan Rossa Cumann!'

But things were not easy for a young enthusiastic lad in a Fianna Fail Cumann of the early 1960s. It was controlled by a group of elderly men who glared at any new-comer who attempted to introduce change.

The Comhairle Dail Cheantair was very much under the influence of an elderly senator, Sean O'Donovan, a veterinary inspector with Dublin Corporation, originally from Clonakilty in west Cork, who was a Taoiseach's nominee to the Seanad. O'Donovan, a veteran of the War of Independence and the Civil War, was a brother-in-law of Gerry Boland, the former Minister for Justice.

'Shut up... Sit down you... Have you held your National Collection yet?' he would snap, as he dismissed the comments from PJ Mara and other young members.

O'Donovan and Mara never saw eye to eye. PJ got very sick, during the 1965 election campaign – 'I had as high a temperature as you could possibly have without snuffing it altogether' – when O'Donovan sent a blunt message to PJ's mother saying: 'PJ is supposed to be in charge of hanging up posters. This is simply not good enough. I will get someone else!'

'In those days you waited 30 years to get your chance,' says Michael Harnett.

Not so PJ Mara, who chomped at the bit. He immediately saw that in order to get anywhere he would need a coterie of friends and supporters around him. He enlisted the support of Harnett.

Harnett's father had been a member of Cumann Na nGael, but left. Michael himself was not particularly interested, but went along to support his younger mate. In Fianna Fail they met an old teacher of theirs from St Pat's, Stan O'Brien, who ran in a number of elections under the slogan: 'Stan's the Man'.

The early 1960s saw a major expansion in the north side of the city, and PJ, along with a few others, was asked by Stan O'Brien to go and set up a new Cumann around Harmonstown and Edenmore, later named the Sean Lemass Cumann. PJ was appointed delegate to the Dublin North East Comhairle Dail Ceanntair and got to know the constituency's three Fianna Fail TDs – Charles Haughey, George Colley and Eugene Timmins.

PJ and friends automatically gravitated towards the Colley camp. George Colley was a recently-elected Dail deputy (1961) and was more in contact with the constituency officers than Charles Haughey, who was already a Cabinet Minister.

The tension between the two men was there almost from the start. Charles Haughey had unseated George Colley's father, Harry, when he was first elected in 1957.

Furthermore the Colley camp was seen as the old true Fianna Fail, in effect, more civilised than the Donnycarney gang, who allied themselves with Charles Haughey.

Already a shrewd politician, Haughey, although a simple backbench TD, hired his own public relations consultant, Tony Gray of the *Irish Times*.

In 1964, Haughey was appointed Minister for Agriculture following the resignation of Paddy Smith. While in this position, he learned how to exploit the media. 'Often it didn't matter so much about the content as long as the image was right,' said one insider.

His private secretary at this time was Donal Creedon, who later became Department Secretary. A tough and no-nonsense Cork man, he and his Minister often knocked sparks off each other.

At one reception for the bloodstock industry at the Department of Foreign Affairs in Iveagh House, Creedon introduced a Captain Wiley to Haughey. Later Charlie called over his secretary and berated him for not knowing that the man was in fact a Commandant.

'He's a Captain,' said Creedon.

'He is not, he's a f*** Commandant,' insisted Haughey.

An hour later when Creedon had had a few drinks, and new courage, he produced the Captain in front of the minister.

'We want to settle an argument. What army rank are you?' 'I'm a Captain,' came the reply. Creedon's face broke into one huge smile!

Both Charles and George Colley were politically very ambitious, Colley if anything, more so than Haughey.

Having been appointed Minister for Education in 1965, Colley contested the Fianna Fail leadership in 1966, just five years after being elected to the Dail.

A potentially bitter campaign was developing between Colley and Haughey, until the latter's father-in-law, Sean Lemass, stepped in and prevailed on Jack Lynch to stand. Haughey agreed to step down but Colley did not and stood against Lynch. He was defeated by 52 votes to 19.

Shortly after the election Colley made a speech in which he referred to 'low standards in high places', a comment which was widely interpreted as an insinuation against Haughey and the trend towards the big business element within Fianna Fail.

From November 1966 onwards, Haughey became a dominant figure in the Cabinet in his powerful position as Minister for Finance. He won popularity through the introduction of free electricity and free transport for old age pensioners. During these vital years he earned himself a reputation for inspired decision-making.

In his office he surrounded himself with a team of able Civil Servants.

'He had the knack of identifying those who could get the job done, rather than the ones who would find a problem for every solution,' says one former aide.

His approach in dealing with staff, as with department problems, was a pragmatic one.

In the run-up to one Christmas a junior messenger in the Department of Finance, who had a little too much to drink, stole a turkey on Moore St on his way home from work. He was duly arrested and fined. The incident caused outrage in the Department where it was felt the erring servant had brought disgrace on their public image. A file on the matter was sent to Haughey. He had it in his hands scarcely five minutes when the buzzer went in the private secretary's office.

'Have you read this?' asked the Minister. 'What do you make of it?'

The private secretary replied that he felt it was a bit harsh on the young man – his dismissal was in the balance.

Haughey took out his pen and wrote on the top of the file: 'For Jaysus sake, have a bit of sense. Anyone could steal a turkey coming up to Christmas, if they got pissed enough!' He made no recommendation, and the Civil Servant remained in the Department until his retirement.

Back in Clontarf, PJ Mara, now running his own clothing business, had little contact with the dynamic Minister for Finance.

'I had no particular connection with Haughey. I knew him, and he me. We met at constituency meetings and socials. He'd say: "Hello, how are you, nice to see you." And that's as far as it went.'

But all that was soon to change. The day that brought about that change was 6 May 1970, the day Jack Lynch sacked Charles Haughey from his Cabinet when he refused a request to resign.

Following the outbreak of civil disturbances in Northern Ireland in the summer of 1969, the Government decided that the Minister for Finance, Charles Haughey, would channel aid to the victims of unrest and a fund of £100,000 was established through a vote of the Dail.

A Cabinet sub-committee was set up comprising Charles Haughey, Neil Blaney, Kevin Boland, Jim Gibbons, Padraig Faulkner and Joe Brennan.

Then, in a move which shocked the nation, Jack Lynch dismissed Charles Haughey and Neil Blaney from the Cabinet over their alleged attempts to import arms from the Continent.

It was one of the few occasions when Haughey wept openly. Mr Lynch brought him the bad news in his hospital bed in the Mater hospital where he was recovering from a much-talked about riding accident at his Kinsealy stables. An embarrassed Jack Lynch thought: 'Oh my God, he is going to collapse!'

Out in Drumcondra, Michael Harnett heard the news on RTE radio. 'There are a lot of reasons for firing Charlie, but that's not one of them,' he shouted out loud.

'It was a very different ball-game then. The nationalists were having the s*** kicked out of them. It was significant that the late John Kelly, for example, never condemned them,' says Harnett.

Over in Clontarf PJ Mara was equally angry.

'I took a very strong view that Haughey had been very harshly treated for all kinds of reasons. I still think, to this day, that he was wrongly dismissed. Other people agreed to something for which they would not later take responsibility.'

'I took the view that a (Cabinet) sub-committee arrived at a certain decision. John Kelly later said he did not know how he would have acted in those circumstances. It was a totally different climate then than it is now. The Provisional IRA didn't exist. These people, the Nationalists, were under attack. Paddy Devlin, later to become a founding member of the SDLP, among others, was on television making passionate pleas for help. These were respected community leaders.

'It was my view that Haughey was treated badly. It was a conscious decision on my part and that of my friends that we would support him whatever happened thereafter. And we did that.'

Charges against Neil Blaney were dismissed by the District court in July, but went ahead against Haughey and three others. The trial opened on 22 September 1970 but ended on 29 September when the judge discharged the jury. A new trial opened on 7 October of the same year.

Every day PJ Mara and a coterie of friends and supporters would cut short their day's work and make their way to the Four Courts.

'We went down almost every day to show the flag, just basically to show some solidarity. Most of those around were his own personal friends and family. Albert Reynolds was a regular attender.'

Then, on 24 October, Mr Haughey and the three others were acquitted by a jury after less than two hours' consideration. Haughey, who had left each evening through a side entrance, came out the front door and gave a controversial press conference.

The Arms Trial made the young PJ Mara sit up and think seriously about the North for the first time.

'Growing up in the late 1950s and '60s in Dublin, the North as an issue had been put on the back burner. And then the civil rights thing started. Events unfolded. A generation of people down here became conscious, for the first time, that there was a problem. Certainly I'd ignored it and got on with my own life because that's just the way it was.'

4

The Wilderness

'We had more fun in those days than at any other time. We got to know more people in the organisation, the personalities and the characters. And, of course, we heaped calumny on our enemies, real and imagined!'

Westmeath TD Sean Keegan was sitting in Councillor Tom Burke's public house in Mullingar. The tall, burly, rural deputy had impressive Republican credentials. His father was in the IRA during the War of Independence and went on hunger-strike for 38 days while in prison in Wales because of the denial of political status.

An admirer of Charles Haughey, Keegan was delighted to be able to welcome him to the Comhairle Ceanntair function in Westmeath. Mr Haughey had driven all the way from Dublin to be there. With him was PJ Mara. Sean smiled to himself as he surveyed the fine turnout.

Soon a team of caterers, employed for the night, started to bring plates of food to the tables. PJ Mara braced himself for yet another chicken and ham dinner. Charles Haughey grinded his teeth, but said nothing.

As the plates were allocated, it became obvious to Haughey that Deputy Keegan's plate was still empty. This was strange for a man, renowned throughout Leinster House for his fine appetite.

In due course the chief waitress arrived at Sean's plate, carrying a giant-sized, well-cooked steak. 'There you are now, Sean,' she smiled. 'I hope it's to your satisfaction.'

'You know something, Charlie,' declared Sean, as he sharpened his knife, 'I hate that chicken and chips you're eating!'

By now Charlie Haughey and PJ Mara were well into what became known as the 'chicken and chips circuit'. Three or four nights every week they would set off from Dublin together and head for the four corners of Ireland. No Fianna Fail function was too small to attend.

Charles Haughey did not like being out in the cold.

For a time after the Arms Trial, it looked as though his carefully planned career was in ruins. He had always intended to be Taoiseach.

In his book *Go And Dance on Someone Else's Grave,* broadcaster Shane Kenny wrote that while clearing out his office in the Department of Finance in the summer of 1970, Charles Haughey told his officials: 'I'll be back!'

For a time he found it difficult to adjust. He began to drink heavily and rarely spoke in the Dail. A rumoured challenge against Lynch in October 1970 petered out, apparently because of a lack of trust between Haughey, Neil Blaney and Kevin Boland.

But first it was back to his constituency. He had moved to his new estate in Kinsealy in 1969 while he was Minister for Finance. There he built up a strong constituency office where he actively worked on behalf of the people of Dublin North-East.

The first test would come in the 1973 General Election. Never before had he worked his constituency so intensely. Around him was a close band of followers, of whom the most notable was PJ Mara.

Mara was appointed deputy Director of Elections in 1973. The Director was Tomas Holt, a long-time party activist. But Mara effectively ran the campaign. It was a difficult election for Haughey who was still on very uneasy terms with the party leader and Taoiseach.

Would Jack Lynch be invited to the constituency? How should the meeting of the two be handled?

Eventually it was decided to have a joint rally of three constituencies – Dublin North, Dublin North-East and Dublin North-Central in Ballymun. Jack Lynch came to address it. It was the only contact between Haughey and Lynch during that election.

For Haughey the result was a triumph. He received 12,901 first preference votes, over 1,300 up on his 1969 figure. His nearest rival, and arch critic, Conor Cruise O'Brien got 7,774.

But Fianna Fail went out of Government, which was probably lucky for Haughey. Had the party returned to power, his political career might well have been finished. But the return to the Opposition benches gave him new hope.

Around this time Charlie Haughey packed in drinking almost completely and concentrated on the tough task in hand.

By now Haughey had time on his hands. He began to accept speaking engagements around the country. It was a deliberate decision to get right down to the grassroots. Start again at the bottom – and work up.

At first an old friend, Dick Murnane drove him. Various others lent a hand, Owen Patten and Liam Lawlor included.

'You had to do a day's work first,' recalls PJ, 'finish up at 6pm and head off to, say, Tipperary, Cork or Kerry. And we always came back the same night. That was the rule. We often drove back to Dublin from a function in Bandon in West Cork that would have finished at 2 in the morning. It was tough but enjoyable.'

The pair always travelled in Haughey's car, a six cylinder V12 Jaguar – Haughey managed to get through two Jaguars before being re-appointed a Government minister.

The routine was that Charlie would drive down, and PJ would drive on the return journey. 'I got the rough end of the stick!' quips PJ.

During the next eight years the pair became familiar with virtually every cross-road in the country. They became household names in hotels – the Hibernian in Borrisokane, the Munster Arms in Bandon, the Sliabh An Iarann in Ballinamore and the Golden Grill in Letterkenny.

As they drove, they would chat about issues of the day, or personalities they met. And there would be a laugh, too, about the fine looking woman one or other of them had spotted! In or out of office, Charlie's roving eye never missed an attractive lady in the audience.

Though they travelled thousands of miles, never once did they crash, or even get a puncture.

'We had more fun in those days than at any other time. We got to know more people in the organisation, the personalities and the characters. And, of course, we heaped calumny on our enemies, real and imagined!

'We also met most of the current FF deputies in the House', PJ says. They also got to know the efficient officers – and the inefficient. The constituency of Sligo/Leitrim was notorious for starting meetings and functions late. Nothing started before 10pm or 10.30pm, ever.

One winter's day in the mid 1970s Charlie rang PJ to ask him to accompany him to Ballinamore on the following Friday night. They had to be there for 8pm. Mara told Haughey that he had been up there recently at a meeting of the Fianna Fail Organisation Committee, and they didn't start until all hours.

'You can forget about that eight o'clock thing, time enough to be there at nine-thirty,' he declared.

'What time does it say on the ticket?' snapped Charlie.

'Ah,..it says... eight o'clock.'

'Right, that's the time we'll be there,' said Haughey.

'OK, suit yourself.'

At two minutes past eight on Friday night, the V12 Jaguar driven by Charles Haughey, who was accompanied by PJ Mara, swept into Ballinamore. It was dark and freezing cold. There wasn't a single car outside the Sliabh An Iarann hotel. In fact there wasn't a sign of any living being. The two men sat in the far corner of the bar. The manager recognised Haughey and offered them a cup of coffee.

Eight-thirty came and went. Nine o'clock came and went. Nine-thirty came...and went. A few minutes before 10pm the local Comhairle Ceanntair officers arrived and set up their admission box.

Eventually the dinner started at 11pm and the first speeches at 12.30am. These lasted for a full hour and a half. The pair left the hotel at a 2.15 in the morning.

The roads were full of black ice, and PJ drove back the long road to Dublin at a snail's pace. At 6.30am they slid down Dublin's quays to the corner of Bachelor's Walk where they picked up the morning papers. PJ went home and had a shower before dashing back into town to attend to his clothing business. It had been another 'normal' Friday night.

These were serious men about serious business.

Charles Haughey normally brought a prepared script to each of these functions.

'He composed a mixture of speeches. He always had something interesting to say, mainly about the economy and the social conditions of the time. But I never remember him once knocking Lynch. He made himself available to all local branches of the party and became very much the organisation's most requested after-dinner speaker.

Significantly, although it was always unstated between them, it was clearly understood that Charles Haughey was carving a clear path back into public life, and subsequent to 1977, to be Jack Lynch's successor as Taoiseach and leader of Fianna Fail.

In 1975, the 'chicken and chips' circuit began to pay dividends. Under pressure from the grassroots, Jack Lynch brought Charles Haughey back onto the front-bench, as party spokesman on Health.

The 1977 election saw Fianna Fail sweep back to power with a twenty-two seat majority.

In the run-up they had produced an extravagant manifesto, largely because they did not believe they could win it.

'I remember driving back from Cork with Jack Lynch and I asked him how he though it would go,' recalls Frank Dunlop, then press officer for Fianna Fail.

'I think we might barely make it,' replied Lynch after a pause.

Fianna Fail knew there was great antipathy towards the coalition government, but were unable to quantify it. Two days before voting the *Irish Times* conducted a poll which showed that Fianna Fail would win a massive majority. However, they decided not to publish it as they did not believe the figures, 'which says a lot about the *Irish Times*' said Mara later.

The day the manifesto was launched, Dunlop met the then Parliamentary Secretary to the Minister for Health and Social Welfare, Frank Cluskey, on the corridor of Leinster House.

'F*** ye,' said Cluskey, 'Ye're buying votes.'

Out in the new constituency of Artane, PJ Mara was now Director of Elections. Relations between Lynch and Haughey had improved and the party leader toured there during the campaign.

Displaying his show business instinct, Mara organised a complete take-over of the Northside Shopping Centre for Lynch's visit. Music, loud hailers, the lot. However, the event annoyed one of the shopkeepers, who complained bitterly to Mara about business in the centre being disrupted.

Unwilling to listen, or be in any way sympathetic, Mara told him to get lost. The man persisted.

'Would you ever go and f*** yourself!' roared an impatient Mara. The man went straight up to Haughey.

'I want to complain about the way I was treated by your Director of Elections, Mr Mara. He told me to f*** off!'

'And I'm now making it official!' replied Haughey.

Haughey was again returned with in excess of 11,000 votes.

In the new Cabinet Haughey was given the prestigious post of Health and Social Welfare. Now a Cabinet Minister, it was time to plan the next step to the final goal, Taoiseach and leader of Fianna Fail.

5

Taoiseach Haughey

'Jack Lynch was a tough man. He might allow you to do a lot of things, but once he had the ball, you could not take it from him.'

Shortly after the general election in 1977, a senior Civil Servant in the Department of Agriculture, Brendan O'Donnell, received a phone call from Charles Haughey, the newly installed Minister for Health and Social Welfare. Many years earlier, O'Donnell became private secretary to Haughey while he was minister in that department.

The two had got on well, largely because O'Donnell admired Haughey.

'What are you doing these days, Brendan?' Haughey enquired.

'I'm working in the beef intervention side of things,' replied O'Donnell.

'Sounds very boring work to me,' replied Haughey. 'Come over here to where the real action is!'

Brendan O'Donnell obliged. Over the following two years this influential Civil Servant from Donegal and PJ Mara were to form a close working relationship that would end with the election of Haughey to the leadership.

'What's the story here, PJ?' asked Brendan at one of their first meetings.

'The story is Brendan, how many votes would CJH get tomorrow if there was a contest for the leadership of Fianna Fail?'

The two took out a list of the 84 Fianna Fail deputies. Some of them were so new they did not even recognise their names, let alone their faces.

Having checked and counter-checked they agreed that the most Haughey could hope for was 12 votes. This was July 1977. There was a long road ahead.

The two men, armed with a mutual interest – the election of Charles Haughey – set up a detailed routine of getting to know new deputies, and helping to solve their problems. But mostly they listened.

Each evening they could be seen in the members' restaurant, or in the bar, chatting together on their own, or with individual deputies or groups of deputies.

O'Donnell, now co-ordinator between the Departments of Health and Social Welfare in Haughey's office, kept a close eye on all representations. In the words of one politician, the main aim of O'Donnell and Mara was 'to find out where people itched so that Haughey could scratch'.

Mr Haughey, in his role as minister, made a point of calling in TDs and giving them good news to announce, relating to hospital extensions in their constituencies and the like.

Brendan O'Donnell handled representations from deputies and took great care to soften negative replies. No letters were sent out to them from the Minister's office without prior vetting by O'Donnell.

But this period was not without its lighter moments. On one occasion Mr Haughey received a delegation regarding the upgrading of Roscommon hospital – a similar issue in 1989 led to the election of Independent deputy, Tom Foxe. The delegation was led by two new deputies to the House, Sean Doherty and Terry Leyden. The two men pressed very hard for the appointment of an obstetrician.

'Let me see the birth figures for Roscommon,' said Haughey.

The deputies eagerly handed them over, delighted to have all information with them. Haughey gazed at the figures for several minutes.

'Listen, here,' he declared, 'an old clocking hen would produce more than Roscommon!' There was no approval forthcoming.

But the young Sean Doherty was not put down that easily.

On another occasion Sean made further representations, this time on behalf of a man on disability benefit who had been caught working in a butcher's shop. The man had, it appeared, been seen carrying huge flanks of meat around the shop.

Social Welfare Minister, Charles Haughey read the cert.

'It says, here, Sean, that this man can only do light therapeutic work. How can you explain that?'

'Now, Charlie,' replied Doherty, 'you should know that down in our part of the country lifting flanks of meat is regarded merely as light, therapeutic work!'

Relations between Haughey and his old Arms Trial adversary, Jim Gibbons – the trial judge had said there had been total conflict between their evidence – were never good. Gibbons was conservative by nature and strongly opposed to any liberal legislation, such as the legalising of condoms.

When it came to his Family Planning Bill, Charlie Haughey decided to set up a committee of the parliamentary party to consider the legislation. The plan was that most ministers would not bother to turn up to committee meetings, and thereby he would be able to side-step conservatives like Gibbons. Through a small intimate committee, it was felt that Haughey might also be able to win over some members who had strong reservations. Louth TD Joe Farrell was appointed chairman.

The meeting was in full session on one occasion with Kerry Deputy Kit Ahern in full flight complaining about the moral damage that would be done to the young people if condoms were introduced.

In walked a west of Ireland Senator, slightly under the influence of drink!

Instead of walking to the back of the room, the Senator sat down beside Brendan O'Donnell, just a few seats away from the minister.

'What's she on about,' blurted the agitated Senator loudly. 'What does she know about it?

Realising the situation, Haughey beckoned to O'Donnell with a wave of the hand and instructed him to get the member of the Upper House OUT of the room as quickly as possible. This particular Senator was a close friend and supporter of Haughey, but nothing was to be allowed to interfere with Haughey's agenda of winning over the support of the deputies and Senators.

O'Donnell returned to his seat and pondered ways of removing the Senator. Suddenly he leaned over.

'Listen, Senator,' he whispered, 'sure you don't want to listen to anymore of this old shite! Come on, and let's go for a pint.'

'Right!' said the Senator, and the two headed for the bar. The persuading continued uninterrupted.

After two years in power, the massive spending promises of the 1977 election manifesto were reflected in huge public spending increases. A protracted postal dispute in early 1979 also weakened the Government's position. Within Fianna Fail a small band of TDs launched a campaign to replace Jack Lynch with Charles Haughey.

The main supporters, or so-called 'gang of five' behind Haughey were Jackie Fahey, Tom McEllistrim, Sean Doherty, Mark Killilea and Albert Reynolds.

In his biography of Jack Lynch, TP O'Mahony states that, unknown to everyone except his wife Mairin, Jack Lynch had pencilled in 7 January 1980 as the day of his departure. Circumstances, including the loss of two Cork by-elections and a border fly-over controversy, brought that date forward. If Lynch wanted to stay, no one, including Charles Haughey, could shift him. Haughey's keenest supporters knew that.

'Jack Lynch was a tough man,' says Michael Harnett, Haughey's Director of Elections. 'He might allow you to do a lot of things, but once he had the ball, you could not take it from him. If Jack had wanted to cut us off at the knees, he could have done it with great ease! But you could tell by his calender engagements and his answers to questions that he intended to go.'

'I wasn't forced out,' Lynch told TP O'Mahony. 'I could have held on, and nobody could have forced me out if I didn't want to go.'

Haughey was closely observing the moves but from a safe distance, leaving it to back-benchers to do the lobbying.

O'Donnell and Mara reported back regularly.

However, Haughey did give an impetus as is evident when he told a member of Lynch's entourage to the States in late 1979 to 'Get back, that man is finished.'

Later, he told the same official: 'What the f*** are you doing over there? Don't you know Lynch is on the way out?' PJ Mara insists he knew of no such trans-Atlantic calls.

But the party establishment were confident that George Colley, Lynch's choice, would succeed. Most of the Cabinet, with the notable exception of Haughey, were unanimous. However, Michael O'Kennedy, having initially supported Colley, unexpectedly changed his mind on the eve of the election.

Haughey's people were aware that O'Kennedy's adviser, Pat Dowling, was taking soundings, and probably sensed the way the wind was blowing.

Colley's campaign was not as professional as it had been in 1966 and he lost the confidence of back-benchers. But many deputies and people, such as Seamus Brennan, the General Secretary of the Party, firmly believed that he would win.

When the vote was finally taken on 7 December, Haughey won by 44 votes to 38.

The Haughey camp were delighted, but believed they lost a few votes on the day itself. Gerry Collins, for example, sat close to Kerry deputy John O'Leary during the meeting. O'Leary had been sick and Collins was determined to sway him to Colley. It is firmly believed, too, that Mayo West TD, Denis Gallagher refused to support Haughey because he was the only Cabinet minister not to go to Dublin airport to welcome Lynch back from the United States.

The Haughey camp were ecstatic with their victory. For them it was nine years' work coming to fruition. All that travelling, all those functions and dinners, all those representations for deputies, all the doubt and the worry, had finally paid off.

Never before in the history of the State had one man fallen so far, only to make a deliberate, planned comeback and succeed. It will probably never be repeated. The role of PJ Mara in its execution was pivotal.

6

Tiger-Hunting

'If I ever go tiger-hunting, it will have to be with Ray MacSharry.'

In Ostan Na Rosann in Dunloe in Co. Donegal in November 1980, a small group of men were sitting together, waiting.

It was the by-election in Donegal South-West caused by the death of Joe Brennan, and the group were waiting for a helicopter to arrive to bring the Taoiseach, Charles Haughey to Tory island.

Among the group were Brendan O'Donnell, party candidate Clem Coughlan, Senator Paddy McGowan and PJ Mara. Senator McGowan was regaling the group with stories of Paddy Campbell of Campbell's Seafoods, and how rich he was.

'You know lads, I hope to die owing a million pounds,' said McGowan. Mara, who was getting a bit tired of all this money talk, interjected jokingly: 'From what we hear McGowan, you're well on the way to achieving your ambition!'

Haughey was now in office almost a year, and what a difficult time it had been.

Despite the lack of support in the Lynch Cabinet, as Taoiseach he only dropped three ministers, Bobby Molloy, Jim Gibbons and Martin O'Donoghue. He had wanted to drop others, but decided against it.

George Colley vacillated about whether he would serve under Haughey, but eventually agreed, when the Taoiseach agreed to a number of conditions.

However, on 21 December of the same year, at a Fianna Fail function in Baldoyle, Colley made a now infamous speech setting out his conditional support for Haughey.

Both PJ and Charlie McCreevy, then a staunch supporter of Haughey, believed Colley should have been removed from the Government. Others who favoured this removal included Brian Lenihan, Padraig O hAnrachain and Albert Reynolds.

The day following Colley's Baldoyle speech, Haughey spoke to Reynolds on the telephone. Haughey sought his opinion on Colley.

'Is he still there?' asked an astounded Reynolds.

But the Taoiseach argued that because of the narrow margin of his victory in the leadership contest he had to try to unite the party, and could not really fire Colley.

'It was a major error in my view,' says Mara. 'George Colley and his faction within the party could never be, would never be, reconciled with Charles Haughey. If he had fired Colley, then they all would have kept their heads down, and he would have had peace and got on with his life and work without constantly having to look behind his back. Instead the disaffection and the muttering continued and the basis for all the turmoil which followed Charlie Haughey through the rest of his political career was well and truly laid.'

Years later Mara supported Albert Reynolds to the hilt when Senator Des Hanafin lost the party whip during the debate on the Maastricht referendum. He told Reynolds he was 'dead right' in the stance he adopted on party discipline during that period.

'It was no time for any serious member of the Fianna Fail parliamentary party to be wrestling with his conscience in public.'

Further seeds of trouble were sown by the Government's failure to tackle the economic situation.

In a television address to the nation on 8 January 1980, Haughey had said that the country was living beyond its means.

Yet rather than tackle the situation, public borrowing soared, mainly through pay increases in the public service.

Dick Walsh, Political Editor of the *Irish Times*, pin-points Haughey's failure to live up to his promise on the economy as crucial.

'In 1979, I remember writing a piece about him saying he wasn't going to be the ogre that many people expected, and that he would turn his attention to the economy. We all pretty well supported his speech of January 1980, but it was Haughey who then went ahead and acted quite the opposite.'

In the Taoiseach's office Civil Servants were feeling the pressure. Back in an advisory capacity again was PJ's old friend Brendan O'Donnell.

But one day, O'Donnell decided he had had enough, and got up to leave. Haughey was becoming more impossible to work with by the day. O'Donnell took his coat and walked out.

'Come back here, where are you going?' shouted the Taoiseach.

' I give up, because I just can't win,' said O'Donnell.

'O'Donnell, when you came in here I though you were intelligent. But you're not that bright,' said Haughey. 'Did you not realise that once in here, YOU were never going to win!' O'Donnell hung up his jacket and went back to his desk.

The June 1981 election was a disaster for Fianna Fail.

Critical to the outcome was the election of two H-Block candidates in Louth and Cavan/Monaghan. Dr Garret FitzGerald became Taoiseach in a coalition that depended on the support of Independents for survival.

PJ Mara decided to try his luck at the polls again and contested the Seanad elections, but without success.

In the Autumn of the same year Brendan O'Donnell suffered a serious stomach ulcer and was taken to St Vincent's Hospital for treatment. One of those who came to visit him was Charles Haughey.

Though in Opposition, the staff were alerted for the arrival of the Great One, and were on hand to greet him.

Haughey visited his patient, then walked up to the matron and said: 'He will probably tell you I had something to do with it, but it's all his own fault!'

Dr FitzGerald's first coalition was short-lived, and it fell on 27 January 1982, when Limerick TD, Jim Kemmy and Sean 'Dublin Bay' Loftus refused to support a measure imposing VAT on children's shoes.

It was a day Charlie McCreevy will never forget.

It was McCreevy's only day as an Independent deputy in Dail Eireann, surely a record of some sort. Seven days earlier, on 20 January he had been expelled from the Fianna Fail parliamentary party. The Dail resumed on 27 January, but collapsed on the Budget vote. A general election was called and McCreevy was automatically nominated as a party candidate without even having to re-apply for re-instatement of the party whip.

Fianna Fail won the February election, but Haughey again failed to win an overall majority. He negotiated a deal with Deputy Tony Gregory, and was elected Taoiseach with the support of Gregory and the Workers Party. Among those he nominated to the Seanad in his 'Taoiseach's eleven' was PJ Mara. His ceaseless work for Charles Haughey was finally paying dividends.

Immediately after the election, a movement began to oust Haughey as leader. Playing a key role was Charlie McCreevy, who had been one of his strongest supporters in 1979. He had become very disillusioned with Haughey's handling of the economy during his eighteen months of office. However, the plan collapsed when Des O'Malley, who was to challenge for the leadership, withdrew his name.

Desperate for an extra Dail seat, Haughey surprised the Cabinet on Wednesday morning, 24 March when he told them he had offered the job of EC Commissioner to Fine Gael's Richard Burke.

'A master stroke, 'tis only yourself could think of it,' declared Gene FitzGerald, then Minister for Labour and Public Service.

But the 'stroke' failed, and Fine Gael held the seat. During the campaign Haughey had adopted a stand-offish approach with the media, leaving his aide, the then Senator PJ Mara to deal with them.

In Ballyfermot, a reporter from the *Independent* approached Haughey to warn him that a major story was about to break in the following day's Sunday newspaper.

'I don't give a damn about what's breaking,' snapped Haughey, 'I'm here canvassing in Dublin West. F*** off!'

The reporter was devastated, on the verge of tears. He was only trying to be helpful.

Enter the genial Mara. Spotting the depressed reporter, PJ adopted his welcoming smile, put his arm around the hapless hack and bought him lunch. He then had a word in the Taoiseach's ear and arranged a brief chat for the reporter. Mara's public relations skills were already blossoming!

But the going got tougher as the country entered the GUBU period of scandals.

In October, Charlie McCreevy returned to the headlines, this time putting down a motion of no confidence in Haughey. Des O'Malley and Martin O'Donoghue both resigned from the Cabinet.

Strained to the pin of their collar PJ Mara, and other aides of Haughey went about drumming up support. They decided to go to Mount St headquarters and get on the phones.

Mara saw a letter of support from a Cumann in Bandon. What Mara forgot was that there were two Cumainn in Bandon. One supported Haughey, the other did not. He phoned the secretary of the 'wrong' Cumann.

'He ate me bare-faced. He told me that in his view Haughey had ruined Fianna Fail, that what the party needed was a change of leadership. Anyone but Haughey. He proceeded to cast serious doubts on my parentage, and went on say that Haughey and myself should be tied together and thrown into the Blackwater or the Lee, I forget which. Needless to say, I lost my cool, and told him to stick his support and his phone where the sun doesn't shine! It was that kind of time.'

The meeting on 6 October was one of the strangest that most of the members had ever attended. It lasted twelve hours and began with a wrangle over whether the vote should be open or secret.

PJ Mara, although not able to vote (Fianna Fail senators do not have a vote on the party leadership), did attend as a senator. By chance he sat down behind Jim Gibbons. Suddenly he noticed Gibbons taking detailed notes of various contributions.

'I remember it well, because he had copper-plate, crystal clear hand-writing,' PJ recalls. Mara noted some of the phrases written down. When the same phrases appeared in the following week's *Sunday Tribune*, under a by-line by Geraldine Kennedy, the Haughey camp believed they had tracked down at least one major source of a series of embarrassing newspaper leaks.

The open vote, when finally taken, was 58 for Haughey with 22 votes against. The club of 22 was born.

Shortly after the vote, Fianna Fail's tenuous grip on power was weakened by the death of Clare TD, Dr Bill Loughnane.

When the Government launched its new plan 'The Way Forward' the Workers Party were unable to support it in a vote of no confidence tabled by Fine Gael. The country was facing into its third election in eighteen months.

This time Fianna Fail was decisively beaten, returning with just 75 seats. Dr FitzGerald led his second FG/Labour coalition.

On 20 January 1983 the new Justice Minister, Michael Noonan launched a bombshell when he revealed that former Finance Minister Ray MacSharry had used garda tapping equipment to record a conversation he had with Cabinet colleague Martin O'Donoghue. He also revealed that the Department of Justice, under Sean Doherty, had bugged the telephones of two journalists, Geraldine Kennedy and Bruce Arnold.

The fall-out on Fianna Fail was devastating. Nobody felt it more than PJ Mara then, ironically, driving through MacSharry's Sligo/ Leitrim constituency canvassing for the upcoming Seanad election. Everywhere he went county councillors told him that Fianna Fail was in disgrace.

Though innocent of the two events, he took the brunt of the councillors' anger as he was seen as a close aide to Haughey. He had to pack it up and go home.

When the Dail reconvened on 26 January, the leadership of Charles Haughey was again the only topic of conversation in Leinster House. Later that evening the place was rife with rumours that he had finally called it a day.

The Fianna Fail parliamentary party met on Wednesday, 2 February but the chairman Jim Tunney adjourned it because of the death of Donegal TD, Clem Coughlan, who was killed in a road accident on his way to Dublin.

The vital few days to the next meeting gave Haughey the break he needed. The old team again went to work on the telephones, while Haughey himself issued a major statement of his intent to fight on. Never before had he been under such pressure.

PJ and party strategists decided that every caller to party headquarters who supported Haughey should be urged to telephone their local TD, or call in person, to express the view that Haughey should remain.

Calls went out asking potential supporters to arrange meetings and get sympathetic motions passed by the constituency executives. Activists were urged to call newspapers and announce their backing for Mr Haughey.

Haughey had been appalled at the paper coverage.

'How do I stop this sewage coming out?' he asked in desperation. 'Is there any God up there?'

But a motion demanding the resignation of Mr Haughey was put down by Dublin TD, Ben Briscoe.

The pressure showed itself on the TDs. A number collapsed, a few were even hospitalised. And Ben Briscoe told Charlie Haughey he loved him! Charlie told Ben he loved him too!

The party press office issued a statement saying that 'any decision by the parliamentary party would be fully accepted by Mr Haughey.'

This time an unofficial leadership race had already started.

North Tipperary Minister Michael O'Kennedy was first off, with his campaign being managed by his South Tipperary colleague, Dr Sean McCarthy. Gerry Collins joined in from his hospital bed in the Mater.

But some of the shadow Cabinet remained solid.

'If I ever go tiger hunting, it will have to be with Ray MacSharry,' PJ told a European journalists' lunch in May of 1992. Recalling those terrible days of early 1983 he remembered how firm and determined MacSharry had been in urging Haughey to fight all the way. Raising his voice a few decibels, Mara mimicked another unnamed front-bencher who, when asked his opinion by Haughey, had replied: 'Ah, Boss, you've suffered enough!'

On the morning of the parliamentary party meeting, tension was rife in Leinster House as deputies and Senators arrived for the 11.30am start.

PJ Mara was in fighting form.

'The bottom line is that you are not going to resign,' he said to Haughey shortly before the meeting. Haughey merely shrugged his shoulders.

On his way down the narrow corridor heading for the lift to bring Haughey to the party rooms on the fifth floor, PJ met RTE's then political correspondent, Sean Duignan. 'Well, PJ what am I to say, can you give me some steer on things?' pleaded Duignan.

'Tell 'em we're going up there to fight, Sean!' barked PJ.

Duignan rushed to RTE's Dail studio on the second floor and went 'live' on the *Day by Day* programme, presented by John Bowman. He quoted Mara's 'We're going up there to fight' remark, which RTE re-broadcast several times during the long day.

The comment brought a remarkable response from the grassroots, with hundreds of phone calls to Mount St headquarters and Leinster

House, all urging support for Haughey. The messages were relayed to the fifth floor meeting room.

Twelve hours later when the secret vote was counted, Charles 'Houdini' Haughey had survived for the fourth time, but by just 40 votes to 33.

This time Haughey had survived what seemed to be the impossible. He was walking on air.

'Take me to my people,' he said, as he headed for the crowds outside the gates of Leinster House. PJ Mara headed home to bed.

7

Senator Mara

'Everywhere I went people demanded of me: What the f*** were you fellows up to? You're a total disgrace!'

Few people have found it as difficult to get elected to public office as Charles Haughey. And few have been so lucky.

He first stood in a general election in Dublin North-East in 1951 but won only 1,629 first preference votes. Soon after he was co-opted onto Dublin Corporation but lost the seat in the local elections of 1955.

Then a partner in a new accountancy business, Haughey Boland, with Harry Boland, he was again defeated in the 1954 general election, having increased his first preference vote to 1,812.

Despite his poor performance, he secured the Fianna Fail nomination for the by-election on 30 April 1956 caused by the death of Alfie Byrne (Independent). This time he got 13,950 votes against Patrick Byrne's (son of Alfie) 18,129.

But Haughey now had sufficient profile, and at the next general election in 1957, he managed to defeat one of the sitting deputies, Harry Colley, father of the late George Colley. This factor contributed to tension already existing between the two families.

It was only natural that PJ Mara should try his fortune at the doorsteps of his own constituency. After all, his friend Tim Killeen was very active in politics, and PJ always wanted to be at the centre of things.

'From the time he joined his first Cumann, PJ felt he was fit to take over straight away,' his sister Marian recalls. 'It was going to be tops or nothing!'

His first try was the local elections in 1974. PJ stood as one of the Fianna Fail candidates in the Dublin Corporation Number Two area. This would have taken in his native Drumcondra, Killester, and Artane. Surrounded by a team of close friends he canvassed hard, and at the end of the day scored an impressive 832 votes. But it was not enough and he was eliminated on the fifth count.

As well as his friend Tim Killeen (FF), the successful candidates in the area were Paddy Belton (FG), Paddy Dunne (Lab), Eugene Timmons (FF) and Johanna Barlow (Ind).

PJ tried again in 1979, but fared worse. This time the quota was 3,100 but his first preferences fell to 590. The successful candidates were Eugene Timmons (FF), George Birmingham (FG), Sean Kenny (Lab), Michael O'Halloran (Lab), Paddy Dunne (Lab) and Michael Barrett (FF).

PJ Mara would never contest a local election again. Now in 1980 a close friend of the new Taoiseach and party leader Charles Haughey, he was close to the centre of real power. He would never again want to return to the perimeter, and would find such a change very difficult. Having sampled the delights and trappings of the ruling circle, it would be difficult to adjust to the hum-drum routine of the ordinary plebs.

But there was one interesting national forum, where you could enjoy all the privileges of elected office, but without the drag of constituency clinics and attending to every broken drainpipe. That forum was Seanad Eireann.

The Irish Senate is one of the most difficult bodies to get elected to in Western Europe. It is organised on an extremely complicated system of vocational panels.

There are 60 members in the Upper House. Eleven are directly nominated by the Taoiseach of the day, giving the Government an automatic majority there. Six members are elected by the universities (three by Trinity College and three by the National University of Ireland), and 43 are elected by the five vocational panels.

The panels have long lost any real 'vocational' nature, and in effect, are largely comprised of people waiting to go to, or to return to Dail Eireann. It is a sort of institutionalised limbo where aspiring Dail deputies can maintain a relatively high public profile, with plenty of time to attend to private interests. The salary (currently £16,754 p.a.) is relatively modest, but there is an attractive expenses package.

The five Seanad vocational panels are: Administrative, Cultural and Educational, Agricultural, Industrial and Commercial, and Labour. Those with voting power include members of the incoming Dail, the outgoing Seanad, and all county councillors. In fact county councillors form the electoral base for Senators, a base which they guard with great care. Daily they can be seen in places like the Visitors' bar in Leinster House courting the councillors and making representations on their behalf.

The election trail itself is a gruelling one that requires criss-crossing the country several times in an effort to make contact with as many party councillors as possible.

When Charles Haughey was elected leader of Fianna Fail in 1979, he had one immediate objective – to win an overall majority in the next general election. In 1981 he came within 260 votes of his achievement. But it was a bad blow for Mr Haughey who now, with just 78 seats, had to stand back and allow Dr Garret FitzGerald form the Government.

Now riding higher than ever on the political ladder of influence, PJ Mara decided to cast his hat into the upcoming Seanad election. A seat there would boost his position and would almost give Charles Haughey a direct voice, in the Upper House. What most people did not realise was that Mara had clearly thought-out opinions of his own, too, which he wished to propagate.

PJ sought, and won, a nomination on the Administrative panel. The qualifications given on his nomination papers were 'knowledge and practical experience of voluntary social activities'. His proposers were deputies Charles Haughey and Paudge Brennan, along with Senator Seamus De Brun. When the votes were opened, he secured 48 votes and survived until the tenth count. Mara remained a frequent visitor to Leinster House, but still without access to the Members' Bar.

In that election two bright, young Dublin deputies, appointed originally to the Senate by Jack Lynch and very much behind the heave against Haughey in the post-election leadership challenge, Mary Harney and Seamus Brennan, were both elected to the Dail.

Their election created two 'casual vacancies' until the new Seanad was elected. The outgoing Taoiseach, Mr Haughey nominated PJ Mara to fill one of the vacancies. He first became an official member of the Upper House on 29 June 1981 and remained there until 12 August.

In February 1982, Fianna Fail returned to power but again failed narrowly to win an overall majority. Charles Haughey returned to Government Buildings, but with a minority government of 81 seats.

The Seanad Election of 1982 was held on 21 April and on 10 May, three days before its first official sitting, Mr Haughey nominated ten members. Among them was the name of PJ Mara.

It was a warm May evening when PJ Mara received a call from Mr Haughey asking him to come and see him in Kinsealy. PJ drove the short journey from his Clontarf home to Kinsealy where the two men sat and opened a bottle of wine.

Some three hours later as dusk approached, PJ indicated that it was time he headed back to his wife Breda, and got some sleep.

'PJ, there's something I want to ask you,' said Haughey. 'Would you take a seat in the Senate?'

PJ blushed with embarrassment. 'Well, Taoiseach... if that's what you want... I will!' The two shook hands, and PJ headed back to tell Breda the good news.

Mr Haughey's nominees to the Seanad in May 1982 showed some imagination.

Gradually, Taoisigh were beginning to use the privilege to infuse some real talent and expertise into the Upper House in addition to the permanent diet of failed TDs.

Among the names were Seamus Mallon of the SDLP, and Northern Protestant John Robb. The others were: Paudge Brennan, Flor Crowley, Camilla Hannon, James Larkin, Bernard McGlinchey, Matthew Nolan, Ned O'Keeffe and Thomas Wright.

Both Garret FitzGerald and Charles Haughey made some of the most imaginative appointments ever to the Upper House, UCD lecturer Maurice Manning points out.

'In 1987, for example, Mr Haughey, made what seemed the most excellent appointments of any Taoiseach over the last 60 years when he nominated people like Brian Friel, Eamon De Buitlear, John Magnier and archeologist Joe Eogan. But curiously they were not necessarily great Senators. Brian Friel rarely turned up, and John Magnier only made about two speeches. De Buitlear was very good on environmental matters, but was not particularly distinctive.'

The appointments are normally for services rendered, and this was obviously the situation in PJ Mara's case. It was traditional that the secretaries of parties would be nominated for a term. Fine Gael's Sean O'Leary and Jim Sanfey, Labour secretary Brendan Halligan, and Fianna Fail general secretaries Tommy Mullins and Seamus Brennan, were all nominated at various times.

However, the appointment of people from outside direct political life ceased in 1989 because of pressure from the Progressive Democrats who, although opposed in principle to the Upper House, demanded three seats there.

Senator PJ Mara's maiden speech came on 7 July 1982 when he spoke during a debate on extradition. Senator Shane Ross recalls how important the occasion was for the new Senator: 'He was very proud of his speech because it was all his own work. He even brought his wife, Breda, into the visitor's gallery, all dressed up for the event.'

He began by saying he was delighted to have the opportunity to 'nail some canards and untruths, and to state clearly what our attitude is to the question of extradition....'

PJ immediately expressed concern about a reference to the Association of Garda Sergeants and Inspectors:

'I am the son of a garda and it was always a tradition that members of the Garda did not involve themselves in politics.'

He then went on to give a very comprehensive and well-researched explanation of what extradition means:

'Extradition is a procedure of international judicial assistance to enable states to obtain the surrender of suspected or convicted criminals who are, or who have fled, abroad.'

Ireland's position was that Article 29.3 of the Constitution provided that the Republic accepted the generally recognised principles of international law as its rule of conduct in its relations with other states.

But he warned of the dangers of insufficient evidence:

'To present warrants for extradition which are solely or principally for the purpose of interrogating the persons sought would be a gross abuse of the process of extradition.'

Old sparring partner Shane Ross came in for criticism for mentioning that extradition 'was part of our mythology'.

'I say it is not part of our mythology. It is part of our law and our Constitution, and is not in any way mythological. All parties from the beginning of the State have accepted that.'

But basically PJ emphasised the importance of prima-facie evidence, and concluded:

'If the evidence is available, they will be tried in this country on foot of evidence supplied by the Northern Ireland authorities and if the evidence is substantiated and sufficient, they will be convicted and put away.'

Senator Mara's second major speech in this very short Seanad came on 1 October of the same year.

The economy was in decline and two Independent members of the House – Shane Ross and John A Murphy – secured the signatures of more than 30 names, sufficient to recall the House for a special debate.

PJ began with cynical praise for Fine Gael's Luke Belton, who had just sat down: 'I should like to congratulate Senator Belton on his fine speech. If he ever gets bored with politics he may well get a position on the morning radio programme *It Says in the Papers*, because he treated us to a fine selective rundown on items that appeared in the press in recent weeks!'

There was praise, this time, for Shane Ross: 'He was right when he said that as a country we are going to have to accept a lower standard of living and that the middle income groups are going to have to pay for services they have not had to pay for in the past.'

But the highest praise was kept for the Boss: 'I have no doubt, with the leadership the Government is at present giving to this country, that there will be a positive response from all income groups and that the people will rally behind the Government in the course of action they have embarked upon.'

Senator Mara went on to reject the suggestion that the International Monetary Fund should be called upon to help the ailing Irish economy. They had, he said, 'plenty to be going on with in trying to deal with the problems of Mexico, Poland and Argentina. They have enough on their plate...'

When he came to talk on employment, PJ made one clear statement from experience:

'The textile industry in five years time will be totally concentrated in south-east Asia!'

And, ahead of his time – or did he know something the rest didn't? – he forecast a future for the financial services:...'the banking and financial services industry is one which is ideally suited to the products of our schools and colleges.'

But the Mara impish sense of humour also showed. Castigating Senator John A Murphy for suggesting a policy of land nationalisation, PJ suggested that such a scenario could see an interesting film industry develop.

'We could have the sort of films that come from the Soviet Union: the heroic sons of the land and the beautiful young maidens having romances on the sides of tractors and combine harvesters, the sort of thing that develops from that type of society. It might provide a certain amount of employment.'

When Senator Mara sat down, he was followed by a future President of Ireland, Mary Robinson, then a Labour member on the Trinity College panel.

Charles Haughey's minority Government collapsed in November 1982 and the first Coalition majority Government came to power on 14 December 1982.

As it was close to the end of the year, the Seanad Election was not held until 31 January 1983 and the new Upper House did not meet until 23 February of that year. Outgoing Senator PJ Mara again sought and won a nomination, this time on the Industrial and Commercial panel. His qualifications were listed as 'knowledge and practical experience of industry and commerce'. The bodies which proposed him were the Marketing Institute of Ireland, the Irish Restaurant Owners Association and the Institute of Industrial Engineers.

It was a difficult campaign, right in the middle of winter as Senators travelled the country pursuing the 893 people nationwide, who had a vote on the vocational panels.

All was going well for PJ Mara until the new Minister for Justice, Michael Noonan, revealed the telephone tapping of two journalists' phones. Then all hell broke loose.

Trapped in the middle of Sligo, the hapless PJ Mara, close friend of Charlie Haughey, took the brunt of the councillors' anger on the election trail, innocent though he was of this particular episode.

Ironically, as he was in Sligo, he called to the home of Ray MacSharry, the man who had taped a conversation with his colleague, Martin O'Donoghue. 'I might as well have been idle as on the doorsteps,' PJ recalls. 'Everywhere I went people demanded of me: "What the f*** were you fellows up to? You're a total disgrace!"'

Everyone wanted to know the full story, and PJ couldn't tell them, because he didn't know it. He returned to Dublin.

When the count result was announced, he received 34 first preference votes and survived all the way to the twentieth count before losing out to Fine Gael's Alexis FitzGerald.

It was the end of a political career which had scarcely taken off. An affable and friendly man, PJ had failed to translate his impressive personality asset into hard votes. Why?

Long-time social friend Senator Shane Ross says PJ was naive when it came to his own election campaigns. People promised him votes, so he thought he had the campaign 'sown up'.

'He is totally disorganised, and naive which is extraordinary for a guy so close to Haughey. And he is a bit lazy. Politics is all about organisation. PJ is also an eternal optimist. He's a terribly nice person and he believes other people are nice. He's not a liar, and he's not dishonest himself. He simply felt he had enough votes in the bag, and that was all he needed to do. Politics is all about organisation and discipline, and PJ was never very good at that.'

'I suppose,' says Mara, 'that Ross is nearly right. And, as I said before, you've got to be fully devoted to your task and give it your total and undivided application. In the case of running for the Seanad I didn't do that. There is another aspect to this of course. Shane like playing around on the edges of serious politics. He is not that interested in the real business of government which is something that always absorbed me and my energies.'

But PJ Mara also suffered from the fact that he was seen as Haughey's henchman. At a time when Haughey was generally unpopular in the country, the average councillor would be seen to be supporting Haughey if they voted for his side-kick.

However, one thing is clear: Senator Mara surprised many of his critics during his short spell in the Seanad.

'People thought he was put in there to reflect Charlie's view and that he wouldn't have any independent contribution,' says Senator Maurice Manning. 'But he did show during that short time that he was capable of being independent and thoughtful.'

People expected to get some sort of Haughey stooge, but it didn't materialise. Mara put his own stamp on his contributions, and had his own well thought-out views on many issues.

The Seanad is a house where people can frequently not attend and get away with it because there is not the degree of attention as in the Lower House. But PJ Mara took his job seriously with a good attendance record.

As Maurice Manning saw it, Mara was trying to break into a 'sort of free masonry,' where others had built up contacts over the years. Perhaps the debonair PJ was almost too sophisticated for some of the local rural councillors.

There was, too, Manning adds, the unexpected benefit for Haughey of having eyes and ears in every part of the House, most notably in the Members' Bar. Membership of the Seanad conferred lifetime privileges on him, and rumours of a coup or unease among the back-benchers would quickly reach the Boss. Mara had acquired a handy extra skill.

8

Uno Duce, Una Voce

'The more senior political writers, the doyens, the people who set the tone for other writers such as Michael Mills, Bruce Arnold and Dick Walsh all had a great 'grá' for Jack Lynch. They saw Jack as a combination of Cu Chulainn and Charles Stewart Parnell. But to me he was plain Mr Lynch.'

Sean Doherty was in great spirits sitting in Hayden's Hotel in Ballinasloe in the Autumn of 1982.

It was the middle of a by-election in Galway East, caused by the death of John Callanan, and Fianna Fail knew their candidate, Noel Treacy, was a certainty.

The Minister for Justice was chatting with a number of colleagues who had come down specially for the election. Included among them were Ray Burke, Brian Lenihan, PJ Mara and a young Dublin woman, Fionnuala O'Kelly, who had recently joined the Fianna Fail press office.

They chatted into the early hours of the morning, and then decided that immediately anyone left the group to go to bed, the rest would talk exclusively about that person!

Eventually at 6am Doherty, Mara, Burke, and O'Kelly agreed that the only way to avoid being analysed by high-spirited colleagues was for them all to leave together. So they stood up, and still watching each other, reversed out of the bar and up the stairs.

Fionnuala O'Kelly was enjoying her first year in the party press office in Leinster House. Having completed a Masters degree in Arts, she decided on a career in public relations and joined the high profile firm, Wilson Hartnell O'Reilly.

During the summer of 1981 she saw an anonymous advertisement for a public relations executive post in Dublin and applied. The post turned out to be for the Fianna Fail press office.

'Had I known it was Fianna Fail I would certainly not have applied, as I had no party connections whatever,' recalls the now Head of public relations at RTE.

The press office was in a shambles. Fianna Fail had been in government for years, and had the Government Information Service (GIS) to supply their needs.

Now in opposition in late 1981, and again at the end of 1982, the party found itself having to rely on its own resources. Two PR executives, Tony Fitzpatrick and Ken Ryan arrived, but did not remain long. Ryan left during controversy following the issuing of a letter to party constituencies which sought interesting 'information' on other party candidates.

To help out, PJ Mara started to come into the office two days a week. He had no official training in press relations, but had been around for a long time. His close association with Charles Haughey meant that he knew the organisation countrywide, as well as the intimate workings of Leinster House.

'I was friendly with a lot of journalists at the time, people like James Morrissey, Sam Smyth and academics involved in journalism like Maurice Manning and Ronan Fanning, both of whom wrote extensively about politics. Editors like Michael Hand, Vinnie Doyle, Michael Brophy, Michael Deniffe and Aengus Fanning in the *'Indo'* were all personal friends of mine, as were Michael Keane in the Press Group and Conor Brady in the *Irish Times*. So I had an advantage in that respect.'

In effect, Mara became a two-way conduit for information. His friendship with Haughey meant that people would contact him to pass on messages. He was as much a receiver as a giver of information.

As the party was low in the opinion polls Haughey pleaded with RTE's then political correspondent, Sean Duignan, to take the job of press officer.

Duignan said 'Thanks,' but 'No thanks'. He also tried to recruit a number of high profile PR types at the time. They all refused. So finally Haughey gave up, and appointed his old friend, PJ Mara permanently to the post.

Haughey now began to build a small team of dedicated people around him.

A top Civil Servant in the Department of Foreign Affairs, Dr Martin Mansergh, a man of Anglo-Irish stock, resigned his job and came to work full-time for the party leader.

The son of the distinguished Cambridge historian, Dr Nicholas Mansergh, Martin was educated at the Sorbonne in Paris and the Goethe Institute, Oxford University. Having joined the Department of Foreign Affairs as a Third Secretary in 1974, he quickly rose through the ranks, ending up as Head of the Energy Section.

In 1981 he was appointed Principal Officer in the Taoiseach's Department, and when Fianna Fail lost power, he left the Civil Service to become Head of Research for the party. A rather incongruous figure in Fianna Fail, he adopted a very strong nationalist line in his work and presentation.

During the brief Haughey administration of 1982, Mansergh was appointed Special Adviser on Northern Ireland, but returned to his old Fianna Fail post between 1982 and 1987. On resuming power, Haughey appointed Mansergh as a Special Adviser in his own department.

Mansergh sought a party nomination for the Dail in his native South Tipperary, but failed. He also edited *The Spirit of the Nation*, the collected speeches of Charles Haughey from 1957 to 1986.

Mansergh was joined on the fifth floor by a retired public servant, Padraig O'hAnrachain, who arrived later in 1984. He, too, was a most distinguished Civil Servant. He had been private secretary to Eamon De Valera when he was Taoiseach, and he was also the longest serving Head of the Government Information Service from 1957 to 1973.

'Padraig O hAnrachain was a wonderful friend to me,' says PJ Mara. 'He was kind, he was humourous and he had a great understanding of politics and government. He also had the most wicked sense of humour.'

They were joined on the fifth floor by Haughey's two personal assistants, Catherine Butler and Eileen Foy.

All worked in close proximity to each other in the fifth floor party rooms. The only other office there was that of the party whip, first occupied by Bertie Ahern, and later by Vincent Brady.

The team adopted a daily routine. It would begin at 8.30am when PJ Mara and Martin Mansergh arrived in Leinster House. Mara would already have all the Irish newspapers, which were delivered to his home, read at this stage. Shortly after 9am they would meet Haughey where current issues would be discussed.

Particular attention was paid to matters that might be raised on the Order of Business in the Dail, news stories that had broken over the previous 24 hours, leading articles in morning papers, or just good old-fashioned political gossip.

Mansergh specialised in the drafting of speeches, parliamentary questions to Government ministers, and in advising on possible private motions that might be put down for debate during Opposition time in the House.

Mara filled in the meeting on what editors and journalists were saying about various issues. He also had a wide-range of contacts in the Law, in business and in the world of the arts. People like Dermot Desmond of NCB, Colm McCarthy from Davy's, lawyers Gerry Danaher and Adrian Hardiman; Noel Pearson, Paul McGuinness and Michael Colgan were all close, personal friends. They gave him unrivalled access and made him an invaluable sounding board. Their views were also passed on for consideration at the morning meetings.

Ever since the Arms Trial, Haughey's relationship with the media had gone sour. A man who had previously boosted his public image through his contacts with journalists, he now largely avoided them altogether. Mara decided to tackle this deficiency.

The management and editors of the various newspaper groups were regularly invited to lunch with Haughey. From the *Irish Press* would come a group led by Eamon De Valera. From the *Irish Times*, editor Douglas Gageby and his team, and from the *Independent*, chief executive Joe Hayes with his senior editorial staff. These luncheon meetings were initiated and co-ordinated by Mara, and were invaluable in rebuilding Haughey's relationship with the media.

In Leinster House itself, PJ Mara began to give daily briefings to the political correspondents, in order to give an alternative view other than that already given by one of the best ever Government Press Secretaries, Peter Prendergast.

Although entirely different in style, Prendergast had the advantage of being very close to the Taoiseach, Garret FitzGerald, closer, in fact, than any of his ministers. He had built up a good personal relationship with the media, and was always available to them, practically 24 hours a day. He didn't tell them lies, but neither did he always tell them the full truth.

'Peter was a very skilful communicator,' says Maurice Manning, 'he was always pulling a lot of strings. Certainly he was as involved in drafting policy as presenting it. He often had a couple of agendas, but his first duty was to protect the position of Garret FitzGerald.'

Mara's approach was very different from that of Prendergast, but they had much in common. At a time when the media were lambasting Haughey, almost on a daily basis, PJ managed somehow to keep the lines of communication open.

One of Haughey's regular critics, was *Irish Times* political correspondent, Dick Walsh.

'Back in 1979 I certainly would have supported George Colley as I thought he was the better guy for Fianna Fail in the long run,' says Walsh. 'He might not have been as glamorous, or as dynamic – and he had certainly made a few silly mistakes like talking about well-heeled, articulate women in the tax marches – but he had a better feel for the party.'

Walsh argues that Haughey had, in fact, got very good press coverage from the time he was restored to the front-bench by Jack Lynch. 'When you think of what was involved in 1969/70, you might think that journalists would have written more about what happened!'

In 1980, while Haughey was still Taoiseach, Dick Walsh was hospitalised in St James in Dublin. A test had been carried out on him for cancer, but he had not heard the result when suddenly things started happening. Nurses came along and moved him, along with his bed, into a private room. Everything was dusted down thoroughly.

'Oh, my God,' said Walsh to himself, 'this is what it's like when they tell you the very worst!'

His consultant, Eoin Casey, came in and sat down in a leisurely fashion. 'Have you not been told?' he enquired of his patient. 'You know, I'm not supposed to tell you.'

'Right, this is it, I'm ready. Give me the worst,' said Walsh resignedly. And with that, in the door strode Taoiseach Charles Haughey!

As a present Haughey brought Walsh a book entitled *Anatomy of Treason*! Walsh asked him to sign it, but Haughey refused.

'He spent about 20 minutes talking with me in that way he talks when he is not sure whether he should be informal with you, or risk telling you things that he really shouldn't,' recalls Walsh. 'But it was a sign of the level we were dealing with each other at that time.'

Next day former Taoiseach, Jack Lynch arrived in to St James to visit Walsh, lying beside the now dying flowers. There were no fresh flowers for Jack, no line of nurses to greet him, and no fuss. But he brought with him a bottle of his favourite whiskey, Paddy.

There were no glasses in the room, so the former Taoiseach went to search for them himself. He was back few minutes later, and poured out two large measures. He handed one to Walsh.

'I heard the other fellow was in to see you, Dick,' said Lynch, as he raised his glass and lowered a large mouthful.

Dick Walsh became very suspicious of Haughey when he lost power in the 1981 general election.

'He simply refused to believe that he had lost the election, and seemed to regard himself as heading some sort of Cabinet in exile. It was then you realised that his grip on reality was not all that strong, to put it mildly. He could not see that a lot of the problems were his own damn fault, and if we reported on them, well then that's surely what we were there to do.' Dick Walsh believes that part of Haughey's problem was that much of the 'glitter' expected of him in the early 1980s, had failed to materialise. Wherever he went, it had to be created.

'I remember him once addressing the United Nations in New York. When he finished, the delegates got up and applauded. Back in the hotel, Haughey was scarcely sitting down, but was rather levitating. "They loved me! They loved me!" he kept repeating. Someone pointed out to him that they do this for everybody. In the same way that continental men kiss when they meet, delegates to the UNO applaud when a guest has addressed them. But it does not mean that they were even awake while it was being delivered!'

Haughey and Walsh seemed to have a permanent difficulty in communicating, even at Christmas, the season of goodwill, when the Taoiseach was doling out presents of bottles of booze.

'When you were there receiving it, you were made to feel he was somehow rather reluctant to give you the thing. He would put it on a sideboard and gradually ease it towards you with the back of his hand. Eventually you would have to reach out and grab it before it fell off the table! All the time he would carry on a very stilted conversation instead of having a relationship with people, and talking normally. He was always conscious of who he was, and who you were.'

It was these perceptions of Haughey that PJ Mara tried to tackle in the political correspondents' room in Leinster House.

Skilfully, over a period of time, he transformed the leader's image by softening it, and by emphasising the positive points. Many believe that in this regard, he worked a minor miracle during the mid-1980s.

But both Mara and Prendergast shared a common devotion to their respective masters.

'A great dislike of Peter's was one Charles Haughey,' says the *Irish Times* political correspondent John Cooney, who succeeded Dick Walsh.

'He shared Garret's view that it would be dangerous, if not disastrous, for the Irish economy were Fianna Fail to return to power. There emerged a certain amount of apprehension within the Fine Gael camp at the amount of inroads Mara was making in gaining popularity with the political correspondents. He was giving Haughey a credibility that they were persistently trying to deny.'

'I got to know Peter quite well,' says PJ. 'He was a cold-blooded fish, but he didn't carry any particular baggage. He didn't like Haughey very much, but we used to meet from time to time for a chat and an occasional beer.'

Today, Mara argues that Haughey would probably have done better, had he made himself more available to the political correspondents. But failing that, PJ resolved to be available 'night and day' to answer queries, and deal with problems political and journalistic.

The political correspondents' room in Leinster House was on the second floor on the Merrion St side. It has since been extended to two rooms, but back in 1983 it was a very cramped place where up to a dozen journalists competed with each other for news stories.

'It was a place,' says John Cooney 'where you got the feeling that you should knock twice before entering. You would certainly do your business quickly and get out if you were not a senior politician there to do a proper briefing. It had a kind of cliquish atmosphere. Journalists like Geraldine Kennedy had a particularly close relationship with Prendergast who used the Sunday newspapers quite skilfully.'

So was there a basis for Haughey and Mara feeling there was a strong anti-Haughey bias among the 'pol. corrs'?

The evidence says there was, argues Cooney. Within Fianna Fail many journalists had great access to men like George Colley and Des O'Malley, and there was concern as to where the constant stream of leaks were originating.

Furthermore, there was further firing power coming from high profile columnists like Dick Walsh and Bruce Arnold. When this was combined with the almost evangelical streak in Prendergast, and the idea, promoted by some of his advisers, that Haughey was essentially evil, then there was a fairly combative strength line up against Mara's efforts.

PJ himself was in no doubt about where he stood.

'The more senior political writers, the doyens, the people who set the tone for other writers such as Michael Mills, Bruce Arnold and Dick Walsh all had a great 'grá' for Jack Lynch. They saw Jack as a combination of Cu Chulainn and Charles Stewart Parnell. But to me he was plain Mr Lynch.

'They blamed Haughey for what they perceived as the unfair undermining of Lynch. Now I happen to like these journalists, but I think that in relation to CJH they suspended all sense of fairness, so much of their output concerned this demon Haughey who could do no right.'

One of the emerging top political journalists to come into Leinster House in 1980 was Tipperary-born Geraldine Kennedy. She had spent her early years with the *Cork Examiner* and *Irish Times* before joining the fledgling *Sunday Tribune*. When it closed down she was appointed the first political correspondent with the *Sunday Press*.

Geraldine introduced a new and innovative style to Sunday writing. In addition to an analysis of the weeks' events, she also began to 'break' major stories. For the first time the public were given an inside view of the often raucous Fianna Fail parliamentary party meet-ings. Her quotes were frequently exact transcripts of what ministers or deputies had said. Her scoops embarrassed Haughey and his aides.

Geraldine Kennedy operated from a small office on the other side of Kildare St, in Setanta House, which she had been allocated by the then Ceann Comhairle, Dr John O'Connell. But each evening she would make the short trip across to the political correspondents' room in Leinster House for the briefings.

When the Government Press Secretary, Peter Prendergast had con-cluded, PJ Mara would come in. His style was simple and relaxed. Drawing on his vast store of gossip, he would, from time to time, regale the correspondents with largely unflattering stories about anyone and everyone, party affiliations of no consequence. A competent mimic, he would often impersonate the hapless victim of his satire. The briefings were largely off the record, except for very formal statements.

In late 1984 Des O'Malley was again in the wars with Charles Haughey, this time for abstaining on the vote on the Family Planning (Amendment) Bill. He was subsequently expelled from Fianna Fail on 20 February 1985.

Geraldine Kennedy took great interest in the development. In the days leading up to his expulsion the political correspondents ques-tioned PJ Mara on the implications. Mara bluntly told them the chipping away at Haughey's leadership would have to stop.

'There will be no more nibbling at my leader's bum!' he declared.

Privately he would admit later that many of those prominent in the party – George Colley, and all those who supported him, those who considered themselves middle-class, respectable Fianna Fail, would never accept Haughey as leader. 'They could almost have been Fine Gael,' he insisted.

Drawing on a history lesson from Colaiste Mhuire many years before, PJ quoted the Italian dictator, Mussolini: '*Uno duce, una voce*' (one leader, one voice).

To emphasise the point, he put a finger across his lip, moustache-like, and goose-stepped up and down the room. The correspondents broke into fits of laughter.

The phrase appeared in Geraldine's column in the following *Sunday Press*, as a last line in an analysis piece about the possibility of a federal or unitary state. The article examined the implications of the refusal of Senator Eoin Ryan's request for a debate on the matter. There was no reaction, whatsoever.

On the following Tuesday, however, Conor Cruise O'Brien began his weekly column with the phrase. The seed had taken root, the late Bruce Williamson, a deputy editor with the *Irish Times*, rang Geraldine, inquiring if the phrase was correct.

'I was annoyed with him at the time, because he had probably not read my article at all,' Geraldine said later.

A war of words erupted between Kennedy and Mara as to whether or not the comment had been made off the record. Geraldine insists it was on.

'I would always have my notebook out to write down what was on the record. When we were into chat, then I put the notebook away.'

Mara disagrees.

'How is it that Geraldine Kennedy was the only journalist in a crowded political correspondents' room who believes the comment was on the record? No one else made a note, it was only a joke. But then humour was never Geraldine's forte.'

A few days after the incident, Mara was summoned into Haughey's office.

'Where did this phrase come from,' he demanded. 'Who said it?'

'It was just a throw away line, Charlie. Geraldine has no sense of humour, she is deadly serious,' pleaded PJ.

'Yea, yea, yea,' shrugged Haughey. 'But, for f*** sake, Mara, be careful in future, you must resist your base instincts. Put a button on your lip!'

But the phrase had been immortalised, and would be linked with Mara for life.

Some time later, an Italian manager in the Shelbourne Hotel was leaving for home. On the eve of his departure he approached PJ, who had arrived in the Horse Shoe bar.

Shaking hands with PJ he said: 'I shall miss my Mussolini. But I want you to know that my family back home were great supporters of his!'

9

Haugheynomics

'A variation between Thatcherism and Reaganism.'

In late 1973, journalist Frank Dunlop got a telephone call requesting him to go and see the leader of Fianna Fail, Jack Lynch.

Dunlop was, at the time, RTE's number two man in Belfast. The next weekend he drove down to Dublin and out to Jack Lynch's home in Rathgar.

Fianna Fail had been in office for 16 consecutive years. While there, they had used the official Government Information Service as a kind of propaganda office. The office sent out all ministerial speeches.

When something important was being said, the Head of the GIS, Padraig O'hAnrachain, would ring around the news desks and say: 'There's an important script on its way round to you. You'll be carrying it, no doubt, on page one!'

That was the the sum of press relations. Rarely was there a press conference of any kind, and the idea of a Government Press Secretary was unheard of.

But in 1973, the party found itself in opposition and out on a limb. With the Coalition in office, a new Head of the GIS, Muiris Mac Conghail was appointed. One member of the Cabinet, Dr Conor Cruise O'Brien, became the Government spokesman.

For years the Fianna Fail organisation had been run by Tommy Mullins and Joe O'Neill from the party headquarters at No. 13, Mount St. They had no press office of any kind and no system of distributing their message.

Lynch appointed Frank Dunlop as party press officer and he took up the job in May 1974.

Dunlop's first decision was to relocate to Leinster House, on the same floor as Lynch and the then Chief Whip, Paddy Lalor. His task with the front-bench was a difficult one. 'There was no tradition of briefing the media at all,' recalls Dunlop. 'Tradition died hard with men like Frank Aiken and Dr Jim Ryan. They spoke, you listened. It was like dragging a dinosaur into the twentieth century.'

But in 1977 Fianna Fail were back in power again. When the result was announced the new Taoiseach, Jack Lynch, and his wife Maureen, invited Dunlop down to their cottage in Skibereen for the weekend.

'I suppose you're looking forward to this big job as Head of the GIS,' said Lynch, as he gazed out over the waters of Roaring Water Bay. 'You're the only fellow for it.'

'There will have to be a little chat about that first,' replied Dunlop. 'I'll take it on one condition – that I am appointed a permanent Assistant Secretary in the Civil Service.'

Apart from the security of the job, Dunlop knew that outside advisers were rarely welcomed by Civil Servants.

'Ministerial advisers are peripheral to the system,' argues Dunlop. 'But if you're part of the system, you can say: "Excuse me, can I have a copy of that document please?" and you get it immediately.' Dunlop's appointment was approved at the first meeting of the new Cabinet, but before taking up his appointment, Dunlop received a sharp lesson. He got a letter from Dan O'Sullivan, the Secretary to the Government, requesting him to go and see him.

'Before we speak at all, would you sign there please, Frank?' said O'Sullivan, handing him a white form. The Official Secrets Act!

Six months into the job as Head of the GIS and Dunlop was feeling the strain of all the Government departments.

'I used to take calls from people ringing up to ask where would they apply for a driving licence!'

Dunlop sent a memo to the Cabinet. More staff were drafted in to deal with separate departments. In future Frank Dunlop was to deal with members of the Cabinet only. He was appointed the first ever Government Press Secretary.

'I believe that Dunlop rendered a considerable service to the system by insisting on this,' says PJ Mara.

'The Government Press Secretary's job is messy enough and hard enough without having to get involved in all that peripheral stuff.'

Dunlop remained in the post for a time after Haughey took over the reins of government in 1979.

Dunlop found it difficult to work for Charles Haughey.

Dick Walsh of the *Irish Times* recalls being present when Dunlop drew Haughey's attention to his picture at Newgrange in an inside page of the *Irish Press*.

'That's a very nice picture,' commented Dunlop, as he scanned the paper.

'Where is it?' snapped an obviously unimpressed Haughey.

'In Newgrange,' said a puzzled Dunlop.

'But where is IT?' Haughey repeated.

'It's right here on page 3 of the *Irish Press*,' explained an exasperated Dunlop.

'Ah, but where **should** it be?' asked the Taoiseach.

'You could imagine somebody joking about why his picture was not on page 1 of the *Irish Press*,' says Dick Walsh, 'but this man was serious about it, and he was supposed to be running the country!'

However, when Fianna Fail went out of office in 1982, Dunlop moved to the Department of Public Service as press officer to the new minister, John Boland. In 1986 he left the Civil Service to join a public relations company, Murray Consultants.

Three more Government Press Secretaries – Liam Hourican, Peter Prendergast and Joe Jennings – were to follow before PJ Mara arrived in Government Buildings in March, 1987.

'The Taoiseach, Mr Haughey, last night appointed his closest political associate, PJ Mara, as the new Government Press Secretary,' the
Irish Press reported on the morning of 12 March.

His move from the fifth floor also saw the break-up of his old team.

Fionnuala O'Kelly went to Government Buildings with PJ, to take
up the position of Head of the Government Information Service. A
new girl, Orla O'Brien joined the party press office. (Soon the
youngest son of Haughey, Sean, was to begin making frequent calls to
the office! The trips ended with his marriage to Orla in 1990, while
he was Lord Mayor of Dublin.)

Now installed in his new office, PJ Mara found that he had to try
to put a brave face on what amounted to a complete U-turn by the
new Fianna Fail Government. Having fought the election on the basis
of economic growth, the new government soon found that they had
£40-£50m less to allocate than even Fine Gael had projected.

Just two days in office, the new Finance Minister, Ray MacSharry,
announced that a planned increase for senior Civil Servants would
not be implemented. The first MacSharry budget was much tougher
than anything Fine Gael had contemplated.

'Internally, within the Cabinet,' says journalist John Cooney, 'there
was an in-built plan that this government would be a managerial team
and far more coherent, with less leakage than that which had embarrassed the FitzGerald/Spring coalition. There was an attempt to create
the secrecy of the 1960s, along with an impression of participation
with the social partners.'

PJ Mara believes the 1987-89 Fianna Fail government was the best
government of the past 25 years. The really great pity, he believes, is
that it went to the country prematurely in 1989.

In his role, Mara gave the impression that there was a good atmosphere between the social partners.

'There were press releases,' adds Cooney, 'containing real decisions as opposed to blueprints from John Bruton and Garret which

were merely visions and dreams, followed by Spring and Michael D shooting them down and a right argy-bargy to follow!'

'I don't think John Cooney gives Haughey enough credit for his achievement in bringing about consensus between the social partners through the Programme for National Recovery (PNR) in 1987, and through the Programme for Economic and Social Progress (PESP) in 1990,' says PJ Mara.

'These were genuine partnerships which were very much appreciated by the Trade Union movement, especially when one considers how they, in particular, were excluded by the previous FG/Labour Coalition led by those allegedly eminent social democrats Garret FitzGerald and Dick Spring. The PNR and the PESP were of enormous benefit to the private sector in this country in regaining and maintaining competitiveness, and to the economy as a whole in the control of inflation.

'It was a politically enlightened approach that no British Government and very few other European governments could implement or even have tried to implement. It was one of Haughey's outstanding achievements and the one that marked him as the genuine, outstanding social democratic politician of his time.'

Mara adapted to his new role as Government Press Secretary with great ease. The morning routine began, as it always had done, with a review of the papers, followed by a meeting with the Taoiseach and Martin Mansergh.

'CJH was always up very early,' recalls PJ. 'He would shower and do some work in his office in Kinsealy before 8am. I could expect a call anytime from him from 7.30am on.'

Haughey expected Mara to be fully familiar with what was in the papers. 'What about that piece on the right-hand side of page ten? What do you make of that?' he would ask, expecting a reply.

Both Martin Mansergh and PJ Mara established a close working relationship with the Secretary of the Taoiseach's department,

Padraig O hUiginn, and the Secretary to the Government, Dermot Nally. No appointment was necessary, you simply knocked on the door and walked in as circumstances dictated.

At all times PJ maintained – and Haughey expected him to – a good relationship with all the members of the parliamentary party.

His first office was directly across from the Cabinet meeting room, and ministers would drop in and out for a chat on their way to meetings. While there, they would discuss problems, whether, for example, the political correspondents should be briefed on a particular issue.

Before making his daily trip to the see the political correspondents, Mara would generally first consult the Taoiseach.

'What will I tell them this evening then, Taoiseach?' he would ask.

'Tell them f*** all!' was a common response.

'But I learned to let much of what he said go over my shoulder,' says PJ. 'Everything was fine until something appeared in the morning papers and I would immediately be told: "Weren't you talking to those guys? Why didn't you deal with that?"'

But Mara made it quite clear to all journalists from the beginning that he was not going to be a walking file of information, in the same way as Peter Prendergast, or Margaret Thatcher's man in Westminister, Bernard Ingham.

In dealing with Foreign Affairs he was ably assisted by a highly capable Press Officer, Dick O'Brien, later to be appointed Ireland's first Ambassador to Poland. A consummate diplomat, with a marvellous rapport with people, O'Brien had a great facility for socialising and entertaining. In addition, he could pursue debate on a wide range of Anglo-Irish and international affairs to a very high level.

The combination of Mara and O'Brien worked wonders with the press, including the foreign correspondents, with PJ putting out the Government's bottom line, and Dick O'Brien giving the explanations.

'I always knew,' Mara reflects, 'that if I needed urgent back-up from any Government department, it was always there. You just had to ask. The full apparatus of the Civil Service was always available to assist in the legitimate dissemination of information. We never misused it for party political purposes; Haughey always insisted on maintaining a clear distinction between the political and the public service aspects of our work.'

As well as his U-turn on economic issues, Mara had to cope with Haughey's almost pauline conversion to the Anglo-Irish Agreement.

'This,' says John Cooney, then Irish correspondent for the London *Times*, 'gave immense relief to many London and Northern Ireland circles indicating that it was now going to work. It also gave out signals to the British media to reassess Haughey. There emerged a growing belief among foreign correspondents that Haughey was developing what was termed 'Haugheynomics', a variation between Thatcherism and Reaganism through all the cuts in expenditure. And given Thatcher's profile, this was of interest to the British newspapers.'

Back in the political correspondents' room, Mara was still holding court.

'He wasn't out to get journalists,' says Mark O'Connell, political correspondent of the *Business Post*, 'but he would like to have controlled them. I think Mara believed Fianna Fail would do a great job if the public and the media would leave them alone. Journalists often threw light on things, and that wasn't helpful. If you revealed something about Fianna Fail, you felt you were almost exposing Mara's weakness to control information.'

O'Connell's introduction to the blunt-spoken Mara was typical of many.

As a student of journalism in Dublin during the 1983-1987 coalition, O'Connell had observed Haughey's opposition to almost everything. 'In the TV pictures I used to see this very austere-looking character always standing behind Charlie. "That's Mara," I'd say to myself, and to me he represented all that was dark and of the underworld, almost Goebbels-like!'

In the run-up to the 1987 election, O'Connell's sister, Una, was working as a maid in Dublin's Westbury Hotel – a temporary summer job. Paul Kavanagh of Irish Printers, who prepared the Fianna Fail documents, had a room in the hotel. One evening, while tidying up, Una O'Connell discovered a draft copy of the election programme in a dustbin near the Fianna Fail room. She thought her brother, Mark, might be interested in it, and brought it home.

The young Mark couldn't believe his luck.

'I didn't think the *Irish Press* would use it,' he recalls. '*The Irish Times* would take a week to think about it, so I brought it to the *'Indo'.*'

There he handed it to one of the reporters, Willie Dillon.

The next morning the leak was the major story on the *Independent*, with the by-lines of Chris Glennon, the paper's political correspondent, Willie Dillon and Mark O'Connell. O'Connell can still remember his delight when he heard Glennon being interviewed later that morning on Pat Kenny's radio programme when he spoke of his 'colleague' Mark O'Connell. The two had never met!

A few days later, O'Connell decided to go along to the official party election launch to watch the action. On the way in he was asked to sign his name at the door. He wrote: 'Mark O'Connell, freelance.'

'Are you the little bollox that wrote that story in the *Indo* the other day?' said a voice.

It was PJ Mara, in person. 'Suddenly I had come face-to-face with this character from the underworld,' says O'Connell. 'I thought he was going to stab me in the throat, there and then. But he didn't!'

Later O'Connell grew to like Mara, enjoying the good, vibrant exchanges with him.

'Very often you wrote negative articles about Haughey, particularly towards the end, but if you bumped into PJ, it was almost as if you had written nothing at all. He might call you 'a bollox,' but he was always courteous. If you met him in the bar, he would always insist on buying you a drink.

'His job was to protect Haughey, and he knew that was a tough assignment. He knew well he was defending a sticky wicket. In a strange way, he would respect your right to be critical whereas the Progressive Democrat press office does not.'

Apart from his daily briefing of the political correspondents, PJ Mara also held weekly briefings for the foreign correspondents in Dublin.

This practice had started back in 1983 when the Press Association's man in Dublin, Chris Parkin, and Radio Ulster's man at that time, Denis Murray, asked Peter Prendergast for weekly meetings. The time was set for 11am each Thursday morning, and ten years later, this has not changed.

The briefings with PJ Mara took place in his office in Government Buildings.

There, at five minutes to eleven the regulars would troop in – Chris Parkin (Press Association), Denis Murray (Radio Ulster), Mary Carolan (*Irish News*), Kieran Cooke (*Financial Times*), Jim Clarity (*New York Times*), Leo Enright (BBC Radio), Michael Devine (*Belfast Telegraph*), Paul Majendie (Reuters), Tom McPhail (*Ireland International*), Alan Murdoch (*London Independent*), and any other foreign reporters who happened to be in Dublin.

The group would discuss stories of foreign interest, but there was rarely anything new to be heard from PJ.

'The meetings did help to establish a good relationship with PJ,' says Chris Parkin, the longest-serving foreign correspondent in Dublin. 'It was always a good social scene, plenty of coffee and biscuits. And good gossip if there was no news!'

Mara was particularly entertaining in the aftermath of the Robinson Presidential victory and he would frequently regale the foreign correspondents with witty tales.

Writing for the London *Independent*, Alan Murdoch recalled how Mara had made fun of the sacking of eight former staff at Aras An

Uachtarian shortly after the President's election. 'Amid glee, Mara voiced uncharacteristic trade union solidarity, he chanted: "2-4-6-8 reinstate the Aras Eight!"'

Later, another London paper described alleged friction between Haughey and Robinson, and mentioned the President's symbolic light shining in the Aras for Irish emigrants abroad.

Reading this to the assembled hacks, Mara – as if a character in Synge's *Playboy of the Western World* pulled an invisible shawl across his face against the mythical blizzard and looking up at the heart-warming vision, exclaimed in his best Galway accent: 'Ah, look! 'Tis Mary, our President!'

Mara proved very popular with the British press. Each Christmas they brought him to lunch, and an afternoon was devoted to saying 'Thank You' to the Government Press Secretary.

PJ, in turn, could be relied on to do a favour.

In 1989 the Taoiseach was planning a trip to the United States, and Chris Parkin had let it be known to PA editors in London that he would like to go. Within a short time a group of them arrived in Dublin on a briefing mission. They were entertained at a reception at the Department of Foreign Affairs in Iveagh House.

'And the Taoiseach wishes you all to know how very much he is looking forward to Chris Parkin travelling with him to cover the trip!' said PJ in his short address. Chris Parkin blushed, but the comment had confirmed his trip. There was no backing off now!

But John Cooney insists that at no time did PJ engage in dialectics or apologetics for the Irish Government with the British media.

Speaking to journalists over lunch in May 1992, Mara explained that, in his view, the British always regarded Haughey 'as a kind of Gerry Adams in a mohair suit.' There was no real malice among the British reporters, but invariably they got it wrong!

But how did PJ Mara really feel about journalists? Asked by Patricia Deevy, of the *Sunday Tribune* in December, 1991, if he had a theory of the media, Mara replied: 'Sometimes I have, and sometimes I haven't. Sometimes I think I have, and then again I find I'm very confused.

'I'll tell you though, what troubles me at times about many journalists is that they pretend to me and probably to themselves that they are politically agnostic, that they don't have strong political views or opinions of their own, that they have no agenda of their own. This is bollox. So many of these guys have very strong views and carry a fair bit of political baggage. It would be a lot more honest if they were to declare their political baggage up front. Other than that I find I have no great problem with them. I like their company, I like the cut and thrust of dealing with them.

'Sometimes I wouldn't be entirely happy with the results of my labours – you know what's reported might not be the way I tried to explain it, or the way I saw it. Sometimes it gets across clearly, sometimes it comes across in a confused way, sometimes it doesn't come across at all! And, you start again the next day and get on with it. There's no point in nursing grudges against particular journalists. Sometimes I do for a day, two days, three days, but then forget it. Life's too short. Some days I bawl somebody out. Once you get it off your chest, you move on.'

10

Your Staff have Left, Goodbye!

'Mara, you've finally blown it! I'm ruined! Get out of my sight!'

PJ Mara's phone was ringing beside his bed at Seafield Avenue, Clontarf. It was 6am. David Davin-Power, a presenter on RTE's *Morning Ireland* programme was on the on the line, looking for a front-bench spokesperson to go the programme.

'And by the way,' added David, 'that's a great interview with Charlie in *Hot Press* magazine out this morning!'

'Oh...yeah?' enquired the half sleepy PJ.

Davin-Power began to read some extracts.

It was the most direct, blunt interview Haughey had ever given, and the reporter, John Waters, had quoted him verbatim:

'....I could instance a load of f*** whose throats I'd cut and push over the nearest cliff, but there's no percentage in that! ' Davin-Power read.

'Holy, Divine Jesus,' exclaimed PJ as he jumped out of the bed.

This sounded dreadful. There was nothing for it only to get to the office first and get some damage limitation procedures in place.

The interview had come about through Mara's friendship with John Waters, then a budding young journalist on the Dublin scene.

Waters was freelancing at the time and had written a number of penetrating interviews for *Hot Press*. Mara thought it would be a good idea for Haughey to do an interview with Waters for the magazine. It would enable him to show another side of his character, be less buttoned down, less po-faced. But Mara got rather more than he bargained for!

When PJ approached Haughey on the matter, he was not very interested. Mara went to the files and got some old Waters' interviews.

'I showed him interviews with people like Christy Moore and Sean MacBride. You know the way MacBride went on wanting to bring peace to the whole world, and how he almost brought about a united Ireland!' Reluctantly Haughey agreed.

'Interviewing Haughey is slightly different to other interviews,' wrote Waters in his introduction. 'First, Haughey interviews you. This, presumably, is so that he can reassure himself that you're not the kind of person who is going to come out with what is eloquently summed up by his colourful Press Secretary, PJ Mara, as "any of that Arms Trial shit!"'

Waters continued: '"What in the name of Jazus do you want to talk to me about?" Haughey's tone is one of wearied resignation, leavened with a sizeable dollop of friendliness. PJ Mara points out that all the details were in a letter he gave him a few weeks ago. "What letter?" demanded Haughey. "You gave me no letter. You never gave me anything!" His gaze, mischievous, but unflinching, meets PJ's head on. HE knows that PJ knows that HE knows in all probability PJ did give give him the letter. PJ keeps his counsel.'

In the interview Haughey said he could not approve of youngsters knocking off BMWs for joyrides.

'"Although, I must admit,' he continued, 'I always had a hidden desire to do something like that! I don't suppose I could say anything like that, now could I?"'

The interview gave a rare insight into the young Haughey, birdnesting, robbing orchards and playing football.

The Fianna Fail leader said he regretted he had missed the sexual revolution for young people.

'"Ah, now! (Laughs) To my dying day, I'll regret that I was too late for the free society! We missed out on that! It came too late for my generation... You were afraid of guards. Nowadays kids aren't. They just call them 'pigs' y'know? But in my day, if a guard said to you 'F*** off', you f*** off as quick as you could!'"

Charles Haughey didn't like soap operas like Dallas, either.

"'I see them because I have to confess that in my house at home there are those who look at Dallas. And, well I might go and do a bit of work, but sometimes I might sit through it. I really think it's shit! I think it's terrible shit! But then I know that that's a minority view. I think most people think it's shit, like, but they look at it all the same.'"

The interview came to an abrupt end when Waters asked Haughey if there was a particular day in his life he would always treasure:

"'Oh, f*** OFF!! (Laughs) No!!! You're turning into a f*** woman's diary columnist now!'"

PJ Mara travelled to Leinster House by taxi, as usual. He hoped to be in before anyone would have brought the news to Haughey. But Martin Mansergh was there, and had seen the interview.

At 9.15am the buzzer went as usual, and Mara went down the corridor prepared for the worst. But he put a bright face on things.

'Good morning. Beautiful day. Everything going OK?'

Haughey was sitting at his desk, his head resting in both his hands. He didn't look up.

'Mara,' he shouted, 'you've finally blown it! I'm ruined! Get out of my sight!' PJ Mara exited without another word.

Haughey was in foul mood for the rest of the morning. It was similar to one morning years earlier, when he was Taoiseach and Brendan O'Donnell prepared to go into his office. On the way out he met Padraig O hAnrachain.

'What's the scene like in there this morning?' asked O'Donnell.

'He's eating children in the raw state!' replied O hAnrachain.

On his way down the corridor PJ Mara met Brian Lenihan, who had not yet seen the *Hot Press* interview. PJ was again inspired.

'Now listen, Brian,' he began, 'you don't know anything that has happened, but this is the story.

'*Hot Press* is a magazine for young people. CJH has done an interview with them, but the way it came out is a bit off the wall. What I need you to do is to go in there and tell him it's great. Tell him that you have read it, that your family have read it, and that you all loved it – "whole new approach", "fresh insights," "generally inspired" – that kind of thing.'

'Got you!' said Lenihan, and in he went to see CJH. He did exactly as he was asked.

'YOU,' roared Haughey, still with his head in his hands, 'OUT!'

Meanwhile, back in his office Mara was having one of the most difficult mornings in his life as he answered a myriad of queries on the telephone to hungry evening newspaper reporters, delighted with this new insight into Haughey. PJ played it down as best he could. But he said sweet prayers for Waters!

By lunchtime, however, the Boss had cooled down. Aides persuaded him that the interview would not be taken too seriously and that this was the sort of thing *Hot Press* loved to do with every political figure. And there was the added benefit that it would appeal to the young. The buzzer rang again, and the Boss, Lenihan and PJ all went out to lunch together. It had been one hell of a morning!

In the press office the daily routine of getting releases out, and answering the never-ending media queries continued. Long term, the plan for a return to government was already being put in place.

PJ was backed up in the office by Fionnuala O'Kelly and two other girls, Felicity Stringer and Sinead Gorby.

'The Boss was brilliant under pressure,' recalls Fionnuala. 'He could be very contrary sometimes, but when his back was to the wall, he was as sweet as pie. He seemed to work on the principle – "I can't push the friends I have too far!"

'But he was meticulous in his attention to detail. Often he would complain about little things, like the manner in which a press release was laid out. "That's absolutely dreadful," he would say. "How is anybody supposed to understand what that is about?"

'If there was as much as one mistake in a particular draft, the Boss was sure to spot it, although it may have already been read by four people.'

But when he was at ease, Haughey would stroll into the girls to hear the latest gossip.

To everybody in the office he was 'the Boss'. (Later when he was Taoiseach, the girls referred to him affectionately as 'the teapot'.)

'I found it dreadful at first to refer to any person as "the Boss", says Fionnuala. 'But it really was a term of affection. It became contagious, and nobody ever called him anything else.'

Sinead Gorby's first week in the office was a memorable one.

She had been temporarily posted in Mount St when she got a call to come and man the office in Leinster House.

A fund-raising lunch was being held in the restaurant in the Zoo and the girls insisted on going to it. Before they left, one of them turned off the radio, which was always switched on low, monitoring RTE radio interviews – but the record button remained on.

Sinead arrived to take over an office about which she knew nothing, and she knew even less about the people who worked there. Suddenly she noticed the tape recording! She wondered why it was running, and played it back. What she heard told her a lot about the people she was going to work with.

'No way! We are definitely, definitely going,' screamed a female voice. 'Get some other bloody one to man the place while we're gone!'

'OK, OK, OK, don't get your knickers in a twist over it!' said an impatient male voice. 'Call over that young Gorby one from Mount St. She can stay here while we're off on the piss!'

The girls were fascinated at the relationship between the Boss and PJ.

'I suppose it was the privilege of friendship, but there were very few he would abuse the way Haughey abused PJ. But PJ's personality drew it out of the Boss. In fact PJ thrived on it, and would come back telling stories of how he had worked the Boss up into a temper! It was a reflection on the quality of the relationship, the way you might "abuse" someone close to you. But both always knew where to draw the line.'

Felicity Stringer got married in the summer of 1985 and left the office. She was replaced by Niamh O'Connor.

Niamh's choice for the office seemed rather odd. The daughter of one of Haughey's closest friends, Pat O'Connor, she too, had been embroiled in allegations of impersonation in the February 1982 general election.

Ever a lover of good lunches, PJ liked to meet journalists and friends in the various restaurants around Leinster House. But he would always leave a contact number.

But there was one lunching companion the girls dreaded – Noel Pearson. Pearson and Mara were old friends as far back as anyone would care to remember, and now that PJ was in Leinster House, the two saw a lot more of each other in the evenings. Pearson often slagged Mara that the girls in the office had too much control over him.

'Pearson had a bad influence on PJ,' says Niamh O'Connor. 'He would say things to him like: "Why don't you sort those girls out and not take any lip from them?" PJ would then come back giving orders and shoving his weight about. We did not like Noel Pearson one bit!'

One September, shortly before the schools re-opened, PJ announced that he was going to buy his son, John, school books. If needed urgently, he would be in Greene's bookshop.

However, within fifteen minutes, the girls got a call to say Mara had been seen slipping into up-market Patrick Guilbaud's restaurant. They were not amused.

'We rang Guilbaud's every fifteen minutes. "What are you having now?" we asked. "Are you really enjoying it?"'

When he returned to the office the girls punished him for lying by allowing no personal calls through to him!

'He often got on our nerves and annoyed us when he wouldn't tell us what he was doing, or what was going on.'

Beneath the surface of fun and good humour PJ Mara appreciated the tough task that they had on their hands, and had to deal with as a team.

'This was a deadly earnest business – the return of Fianna Fail to power. Even though we were working in a hot house atmosphere under pressure all of the time, and dealing mostly with a bunch of prima donnas – journalists, editors, deputies and front-bench spokespersons – we tried to maintain an atmosphere of good humour, maybe as a safety valve. But those women were absolutely brilliant. They could run General Motors, that lot. They were f*** geniuses. They set up all of the necessary structures for the press office. We had the best operation in the country at that time. The Government set-up was only in the ha'penny place by comparison. The Press Office also had a terrific rapport with the front-bench and the Parliamentary Party.'

But things did boil up, occasionally, particularly when PJ would not tell them the full truth.

'Once we gave up on him completely,' says Niamh. 'We refused to have anything to do with him. Finally we sent him a memo: "Your staff have left. Goodbye!"'

11

There's Confidence

'I miss Frank Cluskey, and I miss the humour and the fun and the calumny of the Bar Lobby!'

In mid-1985 a small, unknown group of people started to meet secretly, in Dublin, twice weekly.

Among its members were Martin Larkin, Chief Executive of Saatchi and Saatchi (Irl), Michael Laffan, the Chief Executive of Thorn EMI, Paul Kavanagh, Chief Executive of Irish Printers, Brendan O'Kelly, Chief Executive of Bord Iascaigh Mhara and Des Byrne of Behaviour and Attitudes Ltd Research Organisation. The group co-ordinator was PJ Mara. Towards the end of its work this group was joined by Seamus Brennan.

The purpose of the group was to map out a marketing plan for Fianna Fail for presentation to the Front Bench with a view to the upcoming general election, expected at any time.

Since the previous election in November 1982, the political landscape had changed dramatically, most notably by the formation of the Progressive Democrats.

After the last heave against him in 1983, Charles Haughey had taken a firm grip on party discipline. When Des O'Malley next tried to defy him on 20 February 1985 by abstaining on the Family Planning (Amendment) Bill, he was expelled from the party.

Within a short space of time, Dublin South-West deputy, Mary Harney was in trouble with Mr Haughey. She had the party whip removed when she defied the party leader by supporting the Anglo-Irish Agreement. She subsequently left Fianna Fail.

Then, in the week before Christmas 1985, Des O'Malley and Mary Harney founded a new party, the Progressive Democrats. Cork South-Central deputy Pearse Wyse left Fianna Fail to join the new party.

The party received a major boost in the West in early 1986 when former Minister Bobby Molloy left Fianna Fail because of what he described as Haughey's 'authoritarian style' and joined the PDs.

Their impact on the electorate was unknown and was awaited with eagerness.

Meanwhile, Charles Haughey was planning well ahead for his fourth attempt at securing an overall majority for Fianna Fail. The task was not going to be an easy one.

'The 1987 general election was the best planned campaign that I was involved in,' recalls PJ Mara.'

A decision was made to change the entire team of professional advisers. Haughey himself made that decision. Out went the old group and in came the new – Martin Larkin of Saatchi & Saatchi in Ireland and Frank O'Hare of The Creative Department Ltd on the advertising side, Des Byrne of Behaviour and Attitudes Ltd on market research, Tom Savage and Terry Prone on media training, James Morris of Windmill Lane to make party political broadcasts for television and radio.

These people dovetailed and integrated with the overall group mentioned earlier, to form one of the most outstanding and effective strategy groups ever in this country.

Detailed market research, both qualitative and quantitative was immediately initiated by this group. Based on the results of this research, strategy and tactics were developed and refined, front-bench spokespersons' speeches were sharpened and better-focused (on employment/unemployment problems rather than taxation issues, for example).

Private Members' motions in the Dail were more relevant and better use was made of parliamentary question time.

The research was used to develop an advertising strategy. Advertising on a number of themes, employment/unemployment, emigration, and probably most memorable of all, the health services ('Health cuts hurt the old, the sick and the handicapped') was prepared by the group for approval by Haughey and the front-bench.

This group also developed what was to be the election slogan and theme for Fianna Fail in the 1987 General Election campaign – "There is a Better Way". One man presided over all of this work – PJ Mara.

As well as the strategy group working on the marketing and presentation side of things, the front-bench, with outside help and advice, embarked on the production of a series of very detailed policy documents. This included the financial services, which was largely the brainchild of Dermot Desmond. The thriving Financial Services Centre we have today is a monument to his initiative and thinking. This year, the State will get £100m in corporate taxes from the Financial Services Centre companies. If Dermot Desmond was living in the UK, he would get a knighthood for services to business.

There were also documents on the development of tourism, marine and fisheries, science and technology, food and food processing, horticulture and the development of a national treasury management policy.

The work that went into these documents was enormous and is a tribute to the energy and commitment of the front-bench at the time and to the terrific commitment given by dozens of people in researching, developing and refining these policies.

Prominent among those who contributed were Dermot Desmond, Brendan O'Kelly, Gerry Wrixon, Paul McNulty and Noel Mulcahy.

'That was the best time. It was challenging and absorbing. The result was best of all, a return to Fianna Fail government under Haughey's leadership,' is how Mara sums up that period.

'And no, there was not an overall majority for Fianna Fail. But there probably could have been in that particular election if we had

Setting out… The young PJ Mara on a timber tricycle during the war years

The class of 1949 – First Holy Communion Day – St. Pat's, Drumcondra

PJ and his sister Marian, pictured with their mother outside her Drumcondra home

PJ, as he appeared on a Dublin Corporation election poster in 1974

PJ and Breda on their wedding day – 7 October 1967

PJ with the girls from the Press Office (L to R) Niamh O'Connor, Sinead Gorby and Fionnuala O'Kelly (inset)
(Fianna Fail Press Office)

Early morning breakfast in the Dublin Fruit and Vegetable Market during the Dublin North-Central by-election

(Irish Press Library)

PJ with former Government Press Secretary Peter Prendergast at a Marketing Institute debate in 1986 (Irish Press Library)

Former Taoiseach Charles Haughey with PJ at the 1989 general election (Eamonn Farrell)

Keeping an eye on the Taoiseach at the IMI Conference in Killarney 1991 (Mick Slevin, Irish Press)

PJ at Charles Haughey's last press conference in Government Buildings (January 1992) (Austin Finn, Irish Press)

PJ with U2 manager Paul McGuiness (John Carlos, Sunday Tribune)

Breda Mara (Tom Lawlor)

PJ and Breda on Stephen's Green (Eamonn Farrell)

PJ, Breda and son John relaxing at home in Clontarf (Tom Lawlor)

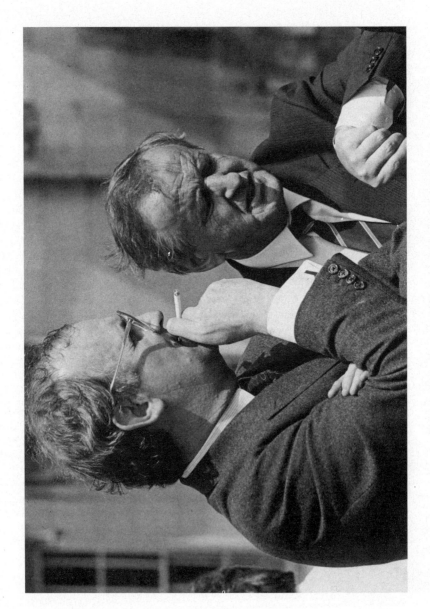

PJ Mara with current Taoiseach, Albert Reynolds (Irish Press Library)

had a candidate-based strategy side by side with the marketing strategy which had been very well developed.

'On the candidate side of things it was the same story as the early 1980s. The party leadership and the National Executive did not impose their will on the constituency organisations. The result was that in key marginals we lost out where we should have made gains – wrong candidates selected, candidates in the wrong locations. It would break your heart on the day of the count to see potential gain after potential gain slip away – Carlow/Kilkenny, Limerick East, Kildare, Cork North-West, Dublin South-East, Wexford – all because sitting deputies and the local organisation would not do their business properly.

'I hope Reynolds confronts them and breaks them. If he fails to do so, there will be no overall majority for Fianna Fail.'

Back in the political correspondents' room in Leinster House changes were taking place.

Michael Mills accepted an offer from Dr Garret FitzGerald to be the country's first Ombudsman. He was replaced by Sean O'Rourke, who represented the beginning of a new generation of political correspondents.

At the *Irish Times* desk Dick Walsh left to return to D'Olier St to take up the position of political editor. He was replaced by John Cooney, a young Scotsman, who had worked for some years in Brussels as the paper's European correspondent. Huge competition for stories erupted between Cooney and O'Rourke as they both worked the corridors of Leinster House. There was competition between them, too, for radio and TV appearances, which acts as a sort of indicator of the pecking order of political correspondents as to who is publicly making the mark.

Radio broadcaster Rodney Rice, although not a regular political correspondent, also began to eat into the political pie by reporting on a series of radio chat shows throughout the day.

A growing series of embarrassments for the FitzGerald government caused these journalists to be more critical of the Taoiseach,
and less susceptible to the flattery that Garret had won from some
writers.

'There was a far more independent line coming from a section of
the political correspondents which was being interpreted in Fine Gael
as pro-Haughey,' says John Cooney. 'By the end of my term I found
the relationship with FitzGerald quite strained.'

The new breed of journalists began to move out of Dublin. PJ
Mara encouraged this and transport – by air if required – was laid on
at Fianna Fail expense.

In the political correspondents room in Leinster House, PJ Mara
was enjoying a great ascendancy in his reputation.

'He always had saucy tales to tell which were totally hilarious, and
which gave out the impression of political intimacy without actual
access to detail,' recalls Cooney.

For instance, in July 1986, Cooney travelled with Haughey, Mara
and Frank Wall to North Kerry, a marginal constituency where Fianna
Fail would have to take an extra seat in the following election to win
power. At the height of the 'silly season' when newspapers were short
of good news stories, the visit resulted in Haughey's interview with
Cooney appearing on the front-page of *Irish Times* the following
morning. Later that year, Mara brought a group of journalists with
them when Haughey visited the three Aran islands off the West coast.
Again Haughey was on the front-page of the national newspapers the
next morning.

'During these years Mara won over a very hostile media to at least
give him a fair deal, and he did this by being very upfront,' says
Maurice Manning. 'He never tried to pretend that Haughey was other
than what he was. He didn't try to pretend that his boss liked the
media, that he was not authoritarian, and indeed fairly unreasonable
at times!'

PJ Mara had also developed good friends both inside and outside politics. While in opposition he developed a daily routine of retiring to the bar after the Order of Business at 10.30am for a cup of coffee with Ray Burke, Brian Lenihan and Labour's Frank Cluskey. There, yarns of all kinds were spun in a jovial atmosphere of *bonhomie*.

On one such morning in early 1987 Mara got a message to return to the fifth floor where the party was selecting its Director of Elections. He was back within 15 minutes.

'Well, tell me, who did ye pick?' inquired Cluskey.

'Paddy Lalor', said Mara.

'Ah, there's confidence for you!' declared the former Labour leader.

PJ Mara was a great admirer of Frank Cluskey.

'Frank was a good friend of mine. I first met him back in the mid-sixties in Groome's Hotel, which Breda and I used to frequent a lot. We were very friendly with that wonderful actress, May Cluskey, Frank's sister, and it was through May that I got to know Frank.

'Frank was for a short time a member of the FitzGerald 1982-87 Government, but resigned in a controversy over Dublin gas. I suppose Brian Lenihan, Ray Burke, Cluskey and myself formed the backbone of that most distinguished group in Leinster House, the Bar Lobby, an unusual collection not united by any particular political philosophy or theology, but certainly united by a healthy cynicism about everything political under the spiritual guidance of Denis Reid, the barman in Leinster House!

'Frank had a pretty basic political philosophy which was that if you had them by the balls hard enough, their hearts and minds would follow! But he also had a wonderful sense of humour. He had a terrific wit in the best Dublin tradition, sometimes rapier quick, sometimes lazy and laconic, but always accurate – and the barbs beautifully delivered.

'Sometimes I would be talking to him, very seriously and earnestly about something – "Fianna Fail this, Frank," or "Charlie that, Frank" – when suddenly I would get the stare, followed by the tuneless whistle, and you knew the game was up. Then the withering put-down would follow!

'He also had an indomitable spirit. When he was very ill and barely able to speak, Ray Burke and myself went to visit him at home. He was not drinking at this time, but had vast amounts of drink laid on for Burke and myself. He was drinking tea and all the time filling our glasses, mimicking a drinking action and whispering: "Get it into yez!" I miss Frank Cluskey and I miss the humour and the fun and the calumny of the Bar Lobby.'

Back on the political front line it had become clear that the days of the second Garret Coalition Government were numbered.

A series of meetings between FitzGerald and the Labour party leader, Dick Spring, failed to resolve differences over proposals for the 1987 budget. The two parties could not agree on the targets for the current budget deficit and the reduction in taxation. Finally, on Tuesday 20 January 1987, Spring, along with Cabinet ministers, Barry Desmond, Ruairi Quinn and Liam Kavanagh, left the Government. The election was underway.

All parties were well prepared, with posters and handouts printed in advance.

The Labour party leader, Dick Spring distanced himself from coalition speculation with Fianna Fail by claiming the party had 'stultified in the grip of one man.'

In Fianna Fail's press office, PJ Mara and the girls were fully stretched. There was scarcely time to eat. Take-aways were the order of the day, every day – burgers and chips, ray and chips, scampi and chips. Once Mara sent out for scampi and chips by taxi. But he forgot the tartar sauce. The girls insisted on tartar sauce with their scampi and had the message radioed to the taxi man, now on his way to Beshoffs on Westmoreland St.

Later, on her way home a taxi man, whom Sinead Gorby hailed on St Stephen's Green, asked her how she had enjoyed her scampi and chips.

'How did you know I've eaten scampi and chips,' she blushed.

'Oh, I heard the message going out on the radio not to forget the tartar sauce,' replied the driver. 'It was broadcast aloud in hundreds of cabs all over the city!'

But, despite their best ever campaign, a total majority again evaded Haughey, who ended up with 81 Dail seats, just two short of total victory. The Progressive Democrats made a breakthrough with 14 seats, among them many new faces including former political correspondent, Geraldine Kennedy, the party's new deputy in Dun Laoghaire.

There was an immediate expectation that Charles Haughey would repeat the 1982 Gregory deal.

But from the beginning, the Government Press Secretary designate, PJ Mara, made it quite clear that this time there would be no deals. The parallel was drawn of the Lemass Government in the 1960s. A period of high brinkmanship followed. Fianna Fail let the word out that failure to elect Haughey as Taoiseach would mean another election.

Fine Gael let it be known that they might consider supporting another Fianna Fail candidate for Taoiseach, OTHER than Charles Haughey.

In the end the crucial Dail vote hinged again on the Independent deputies, Neil Blaney and Tony Gregory. They both kept their counsel to himself right up until the Dail debate.

When Gregory told a hushed House that he was going to abstain on the vote, the Fianna Fail side erupted in cheers. Mr Haughey's nomination for Taoiseach was a tie – 82 votes to 82, even with Blaney's support! However, the Ceann Comhairle Sean Treacy cast his vote in favour of Mr Haughey, and he assumed the reins of government for the third time, albeit with a minority.

Mr Haughey and his Press Secretary, PJ Mara, arrived into

Government Buildings on a Tuesday at 9am, following a Bank Holiday weekend. There was no one else present.

Word soon spread among Civil Servants that the new Taoiseach was in his office, and gradually people began to arrive into work.

In the evening before going home, Haughey and Mara were talking.

'This is a great place to work,' said Mara. 'Everyone gets a privilege day for the Bank Holiday.'

'Ah, yes,' replied Haughey, 'the problem is that a lot of these people think they're Civil Servants in a great imperial power!'

Evening Herald

12

Let's Go for It

'The best favour that Charles Haughey ever did for Fianna Fail was that he brought them into coalition.'

'Are you saying there will be an election?' Deputy Jim Higgins of Fine Gael asked Fianna Fail's Vincent Brady.

The Fine Gael chief whip was aware that the minority Fianna Fail Government was facing its sixth defeat in the Dail over a Labour party motion calling for £400,000 a year for haemophiliacs who were HIV positive as a result of blood transfusions, supplied by the State.

When the vote was taken on Wednesday, 26 April 1989 the Government was defeated by 72 votes to 69.

Up in the political correspondents' room, Government Press Secretary PJ Mara said the Taoiseach 'was considering the implications in the light of the Government's responsibility for managing the nation's finances and controlling government spending.'

The following day Mr Haughey, accompanied by PJ, held an extended briefing with the correspondents where he stressed there should be no disruption to Ireland's upcoming presidency of the European Community.

There followed considerable debate and discussion within the Cabinet on the issue of an election, and eventually Mr Haughey decided to go to the country and hold the election on the same day as the European Parliament election, June 15.

Those strongly in favour were Padraig Flynn, Ray Burke and Rory O'Hanlon with Gerry Collins, Albert Reynolds and new Cabinet member, Michael Smith very much against. Brian Lenihan was ambivalent. Party chairman, Jim Tunny was against, but got fully behind the campaign when the election was called.

PJ Mara was also opposed to a general election at that time.

'Word came to us,' recalls PJ Mara, 'that Fine Gael would oppose the Department of Health estimate in the Autumn. The view was taken that this would be bad for the Government, but looking back, I think it would have been a better strategy to be beaten on that vote, and then go.'

Fianna Fail had clearly not recognised that the health issues had made such an impact on the country. Mr Haughey, himself, admitted it in an RTE interview during the campaign.

'The people had to be reminded about it on the doorsteps,' says PJ. 'I remember Albert Reynolds saying at the time that while most families had no problems themselves, they probably knew of a neighbour, say a respected pensioner in the community who had, and they felt bad about it on that account. Any threat to the health services has a peculiar effect on people in this way, even though they may not need the service at that time. They worry about the future and their families "in case we need it".'

When the results were announced, Fianna Fail had lost four seats as well as two in the European election.

On the Sunday evening when the final result was announced, Fianna Fail had 77 seats, and the Progressive Democrats had six.

Mara was in party headquarters in Mount St when the result was announced. Immediately he turned to Haughey and said:

'Seventy-seven and six makes eighty-three. Let's go for it!'

While Mr Haughey was aware in his own mind of what was about to happen, there followed an extremely long and protracted period of negotiations, as Fianna Fail prepared to abandon one of its 'core values', single party government.

During the negotiations that followed, Mr Haughey repeated on a number of occasions that the party was opposed to the idea of coalition.

The first breakthrough came when PD deputy Mary Harney indicated in an RTE radio interview that her party might be prepared to support Fianna Fail in order to provide the country with a government.

One of Harney's close political friends, Charlie McCreevy, having heard the interview, quickly tracked her down and the behind-the-scenes negotiations began.

'I had often been the centre of attention in the past and often in the wars before,' recalls McCreevy, 'but never did I experience anything like the pressure during those few weeks. Big stakes were being pledged.'

When the Dail first met, Mr Haughey, along with the Fine Gael leader Alan Dukes and Labour leader Dick Spring, were all defeated in votes for the election of Taoiseach. Under a pre-election pact, the PDs were obliged to support the Fine Gael nominee, and were now rid of that complication.

Finally, a negotiating team of Bobby Molloy and Pat Cox on the PD side, and Albert Reynolds and Bertie Ahern on the Fianna Fail side, got down to working out the details of a programme for government. But the key issues, including the number of Cabinet posts for the PDs was decided at a number of secret meetings between Charles Haughey and Des O'Malley.

The PD leader demanded two full Cabinet posts and, at a number of meetings, Mr Haughey offered all sorts of alternatives, including two junior ministries, the post of Leas Ceann Comhairle, nominations to the Seanad – but just one Cabinet post. O'Malley held out, and succeeded in his crucial demand.

So, on Wednesday, 12 July 1989, Charles Haughey was elected Taoiseach by 84 votes to 79.

Apart from the grassroots around the country, there was considerable anger within the Fianna Fail parliamentary party at the dropping of three Cabinet ministers, Michael Noonan, Brendan Daly and

Michael Smith. In particular, there was sympathy for Michael Smith, who had only held his post in Energy for five short months.

But Mr Haughey had overcome an almost insurmountable obstacle in entering coalition, an achievement which he later privately conceded, only himself could have executed.

PJ Mara had been close to the negotiations. Convinced from the beginning that coalition was the only solution, he used his close friendship with Charlie McCreevy to maintain the lines of contact with the PDs.

'Mara is one of the shrewdest men I know,' says McCreevy. 'If Haughey listened to him more often, he would have been more successful. But he was always loyal to Haughey, although he would sometimes know that he was wrong.'

'There was a lot of bullshit talked during those negotiations by all sorts of people,' says Mara. 'What Haughey got was coalition on the cheapest possible terms. It is a basic fact that a minority party going into coalition always gets disproportionate number of Cabinet seats. It is always the way. There was never any question in my mind but that the Progressive Democrats had to get two full Cabinet seats from their six deputies.'

PJ Mara was also struck by the way Haughey and O'Malley – traditional foes – got on so well during the negotiations. 'It was one of those strange things that happen in life,' he admits. 'But then I suppose the PDs are, more or less, part of the extended Fianna Fail family!'

He gets quite angry at allegations that Charles Haughey had 'sold out' on Fianna Fail's core value in order to keep himself in power.

'One of the great myths of modern Irish politics is that Charles Haughey was a failure because he never got an overall majority in a General Election. In the future an overall majority will be achieved only once in six elections. The reality is that Haughey held the party vote at 44 per cent through thick and thin – the rise of Garret

FitzGerald and Fine Gael in the early 1980s, a breakaway party, and in more recent years, the resurgence of the left.

'When Jack Lynch got an overall majority in 1977 there were no PDs, the Workers Party did not exist and the Labour Party was demoralised. Most important of all, after 1977 the revision of constituency boundaries was taken from the political parties and given to an independent commission.'

According to Mara, if Albert Reynolds gets an overall majority, it will be because the left is so fragmented and Fine Gael are 'in bits'. Thereafter, it will be back to coalitions.

'The best favour that Charles Haughey ever did for Fianna Fail was that he brought them into coalition. Coalition is now an option for any future Fianna Fail leader. He has ensured for the foreseeable future, because of the fragmentation of the opposition groupings, that Fianna Fail will be in Government on its own, or with the support of a minority party. If he had given into what the headbangers in Fianna Fail wanted, then the party would have gone off into the wilderness, and could now conceivably be in the position that Fine Gael finds itself and the people would be questioning the relevance of Fianna Fail!

'In 1982 Fine Gael had nearly 40 per cent of the vote. Haughey's reputation was at an all-time low and the party was in disarray. We had lost the December 1982 general election followed by the loss of Dublin West in the by-election to replace Dick Burke. The FG/Labour coalition was well established with a comfortable, working majority in the Dail, was respected and popular with the public.

'Then the Labour Party blew what could have been the natural order of things for years to come – a FG/Labour coalition. Now a major question mark hangs over Fine Gael. I don't believe that party has a leadership problem. I believe they have a relevance problem.'

Fine Gael Senator Maurice Manning argues that by 1989 the media had begun to regard Mara as someone who was much brighter than the sort of clown prince he portrayed.

'He is someone who has an extraordinary good grasp of complex issues. He could get to the nub of any argument very quickly. He displayed a great common sense which he could apply to almost any issue. He also had the capacity to win over the out-of-town media, many of whom had regarded him in the past, without knowing him, as some sort of cowboy or thug.'

Nowhere was Mara regarded with greater suspicion than in Cork, and in particular, in the *Cork Examiner* newsroom, where there was huge resentment at Haughey's failure to re-appoint a deputy from the county to the Cabinet. Editorial after editorial berated the Taoiseach for this unforgiveable 'oversight'.

Despite Haughey's apparent antipathy to Cork, Mara managed to maintain a good relationship with the journalists at the *Cork Examiner.*

Mara, according to *Cork Examiner* journalist TP O'Mahony, helped to temper Haughey's antipathy at times, not least where the press were concerned.

'Charlie felt that Cork had it in for him because of his role in ousting Jack Lynch – and in the end he wrote the place off in electoral terms.'

This led to a perception in Cork that the region was being deliberately neglected, not least by being denied representation at the Cabinet table.

PJ's response to this – no doubt echoing Charlie – was: 'F*** OFF!'

He would respond to complaints with the rejoinder: 'You had a bunch of whingers down there. And you better face the fact that you'll get nothing from Haughey – and that's official.'

Haughey was also frequently needled by the editorials in the *Examiner,* and Mara was the conduit through which these complaints were passed on.

'I see you f****** are sniping at CJH again,' was a typical comment. Then, in the next breath he would add: 'Sure, he doesn't give a

damn about the *Examiner* anyway, or Cork for that matter. Cop your-
selves on....'

But behind the colourful bluster, or the barrage of expletives, PJ
Mara – unlike his Boss – had a genuine affection for Cork. He liked
the city, and the local humour and in particular, Cork songs.

At the Ogra Fianna Fail Annual Conference in FitzPatrick's Silver
Springs Hotel in Cork in the Autumn of 1991 Mara refused to go to
bed until TP O'Mahony sang 'The Boys of Fairhill' for him.

Neither did he ever bear a grudge against an individual journalist,
or try to be vindictive.

Reporters rushing for deadlines for the *Evening Echo* could rely on
PJ to give them a steer, however vague, on the particular issue of the
day.

Mara himself defends – well he would, wouldn't he – Haughey's
attitude to the southern capital.

'When he first came to power, he promoted Gene FitzGerald to
the full cabinet. He did not rate the other deputies there much in
terms of ability. He didn't rate Joe Walsh for some reason or other. It
was simply a matter of personnel, and how CJH rated them.'

Mara further points out that Fianna Fail already have 8 out of 20
seats in the county. The most they could hope for would be an extra
two – Cork North-West at a push and maybe one in the city. But never
in Cork South-West, Minister Joe Walsh's constituency.

'It's Michael Collins country, traditional Fine Gael, and Cork
North-West is much the same,' he concludes.

For PJ Mara in the aftermath of the 1989 general election, everything changed and nothing changed.

Unlike most government press secretaries, who regarded themselves as Civil Servants, and remained at a distance from the
nitty-gritty of party politics, PJ Mara was always in the thick of things.

During the election he had joined the girls again in the party press
office, helping to get out the scripts and providing people for interviews.

But he was always in good spirits and the banter resumed in the office, as of old. But PJ went out to lunch almost every day, again to the chagrin of the girls.

'He would stroll boldly back into the office after lunch. But sometimes he would bring back a bag full from a take-away and go around the room dividing up the goodies, singing: "Who loves you, baby?" says Niamh O'Connor.

Back in Government Buildings he was joined by Stephen O'Byrnes of the PDs, who was appointed Assistant Government Press Secretary to look after the interests of Des O'Malley, Bobby Molloy and Mary Harney.

'Stephen and I got on just fine,' says PJ. 'He got on with his business and I got on with mine.'

Mara had little difficulty in adapting to the new personnel in government. In the late 1980s he had developed good relations with Des O'Malley around Leinster House. He had also worked closely with Mary Harney during the negotiations for coalition.

Harney has immense respect for Mara, and in an interview in 1986, credited him with 'bringing Fianna Fail back into Doheny and Nesbitts, the watering hole of academics on Dublin's Baggot St.'

But Mara was never particularly close to Bobby Molloy, and the two share little in common.

Back in Government, Charles Haughey was now President of the European Community for the first six months of 1990. The task gave added responsibility to PJ, who equally enjoyed the cut and thrust of dealing with the foreign media.

On one occasion, in the Abbey Tavern in Howth, Co. Dublin, PJ was entertaining a group of Canadian journalists, who had accompanied Prime Minister Brian Mulrooney to Dublin. There were a few Irish journalists invited, including Tara Buckley, political reporter with the Evening Press. 'Excuse me, sir,' asked one curious reporter of Mara. 'Are you a government minister?'

'No, I'm not a minister, I tell lies on behalf of ministers!' quipped PJ.

Asked what the 'PJ' stood for, Mara replied that everyone knew him simply as 'PJ,' except his regular taxi-driver who called him 'Paddy'.

'But,' says *Sunday Independent* journalist and close Mara confidant, Sam Smyth, 'anyone who is known by their initials rather than by their name automatically has a more serious, awesome front. A fellow known as "PJ" is taken far more seriously than a fellow known as simply "Paddy!"'

Writing in the same newspaper, journalist Declan Lynch noted that 'those who have seen him briefing foreign journalists on the intricacies of the economy have been highly impressed at his command of detail, and he is particularly good at gobbling up British tabloid hacks and sending them home to Wapping in bite-sized pieces.

'Journalists can come away from 'pow-wow' with PJ feeling they have been given a searing insight into the very soul of the government, only to discover that much of their info. is unusable either for reasons of libel or public decency!'

Lynch pointed out that Mara loved acting the fool, which did not necessarily mean that he was one. Indeed the sophistication of his media techniques was quite daunting.

'There would be a buzz in the political correspondents' room in Leinster House when PJ came in,' recalls *Irish Press* political correspondent, Emily O'Reilly. 'There would follow a litany of atrocious gossip about who was having it off with whom. There would be a bit of a circus thrown in, funny walks, and funny voices. You were left with a benign impression of Mara, which to a degree translated into a benign impression of Haughey.'

The *Five o'clock follies,* is how Maol Muire Tynan of the *Irish Times,* describes the briefings of 1990 and 1991.

'He was like a rubber wall when it came to information. You could stay running against him, but you would never knock him. It was impossible to get information, and anything he said was what Haughey wanted you to know.

'He would sail in the door, always impeccably groomed, smoking a cigarette, great elegance about him. Then he would sit down in this non-chalant, debonair way and throw one leg over the other.

'"Did you know that Mrs Mara is not pleased with me...?" he would begin, as he launched into some highly-colourful tale from the previous evening's shenanigans in the Horse Shoe bar, or wherever. Much of it was unrepeatable, but it provided a tasty morsel for the political correspondents, and it never went any further.'

Mara's frivolity and play-acting with female reporters knew no bounds. He developed a particular fondness for Miriam Lord, a very good sketch writer with the *Irish Independent*.

Miriam was wont to continually turn up in a pair of Levis, so at the 1990 Ard Fheis PJ promised her £20 if she would come in on the following day, dressed in a skirt. Miriam agreed, and Justice Minister Ray Burke supervised the handing over of the notes! A photograph was taken to record the event for posterity.

When abroad on trips with Haughey, Mara entertained with equal, if not more, *bonhomie* and goodwill. And the stories rolled on.

But he could be tough and brutal to opponents if he wished, particularly if the Taoiseach's or the Government's interests were in any way threatened.

At a European Council meeting in Rhodes in December 1988 there was great anticipation of a row between the British Prime Minister, Margaret Thatcher and the Taoiseach, Charles Haughey over the handling of the extradition of Fr Paddy Ryan. At the time Haughey was recovering from a very serious respiratory illness.

When the Irish delegation arrived in Rhodes, they found that Downing St had informed the British media representatives that a meeting was scheduled between the Taoiseach and the British PM for 10am the following morning. It was the first the Irish had heard of it.

All the talk among the British journalists and commentators was of the 'handbagging' that Thatcher would give to 'that awful man Hockey!'

PJ Mara heard all of this and duly informed the Taoiseach.

There and then Haughey told PJ that 'there will be no meeting in the morning at 10am or any other time unless it is arranged in a proper fashion.'

'What will I tell the press?' inquired PJ.

'Tell them whatever you like!' replied Haughey.

Mara called an impromptu press conference and told the assembled journalists that the meeting Bernard Ingham had spoken of would not now take place.

'Why?' snapped one curious reporter.

'For reasons of personal convenience,' replied Mara.

'Whose convenience?' queried the intrepid reporter.

'Mr Haughey's, of course!' said a delighted Mara, grinning from ear to ear.

Mara continued to play ducks and drakes with his British counterpart all that weekend.

The meeting eventually took place at a time suggested by the Irish side, and agreed to by the British delegation, and all was sweetness and light. There was no handbagging!

13
Breda

'It was love at first bite!'

In the Spring of 1964 the Minister for Justice, Charles Haughey addressed a Fianna Fail gathering in the Hollybrook Hotel in Clontarf.

Before he rose to speak, his roving eyes spotted an attractive, young woman in the front row. Dark-haired, and wearing a smart green trouser suit, Haughey caught her attention and winked at her. The woman blushed.

'Things are looking up for Fianna Fail!' said the Justice Minister, as he began his address.

The woman's name was Breda Brogan, a native of Kinvara, a beautiful seaside village in Co. Galway. Breda was the fifth in a family of fourteen children. This was only her third date with PJ Mara, and it had begun, as many more dates would, with a Fianna Fail meeting.

Breda Brogan, a garda's daughter, had first seen PJ Mara at a wedding in the Great Southern Hotel in Galway on 14 August 1963.

Then 22 years old, PJ was on a holiday with his uncles in Oughterard, and was supposed to go on a trip to Knock shrine with a Dublin group.

However, he had dodged the pilgrimage by not turning up at the appointed place and instead, headed for the Great Southern Hotel where his Drumcondra friend, Michael Harnett, was at a cousin's wedding. Paddy Egan, a cousin of Michael's was marrying Breda's sister, Anne, and Breda was the bridesmaid.

'I remember seeing him coming into the room wearing an old mac, not a particularly impressive sight,' says Breda.

The young Mara surveyed the hall and spotted the good-looking woman in the satin dress.

'Michael, you must arrange an introduction for me when we get back to Dublin,' he said, noting with some concern that Breda Brogan was accompanied by a boyfriend.

The meeting took place at a Christmas party the same year in Paddy Egan's late mother's house on the North Circular Road. This time Breda came alone. The two became an item immediately.

'I don't think he ever had any other real girlfriend,' says PJ's sister Marian. 'Certainly Breda was the only one he ever brought home. He thought it would help that she was from Galway, his mother's native county. But for years afterwards, Sabina Mara used to (jokingly) blame Michael Harnett for stealing her son from her!

Breda Brogan was working in a number of capacities in Dublin, and living in a flat on St Peter's Road on the north side of the city.

For a while she taught typing at Rosses College on the Green, as well as doing part-time modelling and hair-dressing.

Oscar-winning producer, Noel Pearson can still remember seeing her at her hair-dressing work:

'PJ would never be far away, he was a right dazzler at the time!'

Was it love at first sight? 'It was more like love at first bite!' quips PJ, who admits they became inseparable.

On 18 January 1964, he proposed to Breda, in a hand-written note (which she still has) in the Bailey pub in Duke St. Breda accepted, but it was to be a further three years before the couple got married.

During this time Breda had been a part-time model with the Miriam Woodbyrn agency, and then with Betty Whelan. However, PJ resented this side of her career, particularly when she was away from Dublin for days. Eventually she gave it up, at his insistence.

The couple were married in Kinvara on 7 October 1967. The reception was held at the Great Southern Hotel in Galway. 'We had our friends down from all over the country for the occasion.'

When it came to honeymoon time, the newly weds tried to pull a fast one.

'We told all our friends we were going to Jury's in Cork, but we had no money at the time. So we slipped quietly back to Dublin where we had a beautiful flat on Raglan Road. We hired a black and white telly and stayed in during the day, only slipping out to eat at night. However, we were caught by Breda's brother-in-law, Paddy Egan, who spotted us in town late one night!'

The couple left Raglan Road, and moved to nearby Waterloo Road, before finally buying a house on Seafield Avenue, Clontarf in 1971. It cost £8,000.

They remained there for 21 years before moving to their present home.

The young Breda Brogan was by now involved in a new money-making venture, this time a mail order business where she advertised clothes on the Sunday newspapers and then mailed them to customers the following week. The business expanded so well that the Maras decided to get in their own machinists and make the garments themselves.

Drawing on her modelling skills, Breda modelled the outfits herself. The picture would appear in the Sunday papers offering the garment in a range of sizes. By Tuesday the orders would start flowing in.

So emerged Bee Line, the clothing company which PJ named after his wife. She continued to work there until they finally sold out to Penneys.

The Mara's only son, John, was born in 1973 in the Rotunda Hospital. 'It was the happiest day of my life, giving birth to my son,' recalls Breda. 'PJ was absolutely over the moon and filled the entire hospital with flowers.'

Money was never a prime consideration with either PJ or Breda. It was something you needed to get by, and somehow they always managed.

As PJ became almost a full-time associate of Charles Haughey, Breda found herself more and more on her own.

'I coped,' she recalls. 'I had to get used to it and I realised the demands of the job were such that I had to take a back seat.'

Politics spilled over into No. 23 Seafield Avenue, particularly at election time. Like many other housewives, Breda Mara became an unpaid political secretary for Fianna Fail.

When he ran for the local elections in 1974 and 1979, she got fully involved in the electioneering.

In the 1979 elections, which coincided with the European elections, Director of Elections in Dublin North-Central, Michael Harnett got an idea. To save expense he asked a 'back street' printer to print the heads of the local election candidates on the back of the European leaflets, which had been supplied free. The result was dreadful.

When a strategy meeting was called, Breda Mara represented her husband.

'These hand-outs are absolutely awful,' she declared to the unsuspecting gathering. 'Nobody would vote for anybody in those photographs.'

The chairman of the meeting, Michael Harnett was in a dilemma.

'I simply could not throw away 30,000 free leaflets,' he recalls. 'I had to face her down and promise that we would print some better ones as well. But we were all surprised at the normally shy, and retiring Breda. I was very impressed at the way she stood up for PJ.'

Breda Mara knows of no happier man than PJ.

'He is simply the happiest man I know. Of course we have rows – they don't last long, PJ could never bear a grudge.

'I am not a morning person, so generally PJ and John have left the house by the time I get up. We have always found this to be the best formula for a friction-free relationship!'

PJ leaves her short personal notes, often in verse, in which he describes his love for her and Breda has collected these over the years. Some – the less salacious ones – are pinned on the wall, above the fireplace in the kitchen.

PJ loves Breda's popularity as much as he enjoys his own. When you mention her, he smiles appreciably and asks: 'Have you met her? Isn't she beautiful?'

Sometimes when he introduces Breda, he adopts mock biblical language, and enquires: 'Have you met my beloved wife in whom I am well pleased?'

But PJ Mara is not a dab-hand around the house. He has never been known to mow the lawn or plant a shrub of any kind. Recently Breda sent him out to the garage to do a small job. Within minutes he was back.

'Breda,' he shouted, 'where is the bloody light switch in that garage?'

'Where do think it is?' she snapped back. 'It's in the very same place as it has been for the past 21 years!'

'You should have seen him,' says Breda, 'he had both his hands up in the air as if he had been contaminated by something!'

To relax, the Maras go on holidays to Kinvara in Galway, or abroad to Cape Cod or the South of France. 'When PJ was in politics we liked to get as far away as possible,' claims Breda.

In Kinvara, PJ's favourite pastime is to sit on the pier across from Connolly's pub with a book.

There he will while away the hours enjoying the view while Connollys ferry him across a supply of good pints!

The family is currently building a holiday home in Kinvara, with a direct view out over the sea.

PJ Mara doesn't swim, nor will he go for a trip in his brother-in-law's hooker, but there is nowhere he is happier than in Kinvara or touring the west coast between Ballyvaughan and Connemara.

The year 1992 was not a good year for Breda. In January she began to feel unwell.

'It was nothing', the doctors said, and 'would soon pass away'.

But the pain did not go away, in fact it got worse. Breda could stand it no longer. She was taken in for a scan.

A tumour on the kidney was diagnosed. Worse still, it was malignant. Their world nearly fell apart. PJ Mara was told the bad news on his car telephone as he drove home from Shannon. He was stunned.

'It is 100 miles from Roscrea, where I got the call from the doctor, to Dublin,' says PJ. 'That was the worst 100 miles I have ever travelled – the worst journey of my life.'

He arrived at the Mater Hospital in a dreadful state. Breda will never forget how pale he looked. They were both shattered.

The following day the surgeons removed the cancerous kidney. The results were excellent and Breda was given a clean bill of health.

'I just feel so grateful to God that I was diagnosed on time and consider muself to be very lucky. I did not have to have chemotherapy, or any other treatment except to report back to the surgeon every few months.

'But you never know,' insists Breda. 'There is always the danger it can spread. It's something you have to put to the back of your mind in order to stay sane.'

The recovery was tiring and painful. Worse still, her doctor had ordered her to stop smoking – she had given up alcohol completely in 1979.

But her illness and PJ's new job, has brought them closer together. Now they go out more together and share more time with each other, and with their son, John.

'Breda is gentle, loyal and intelligent. She is a wonderful ally and a formidable foe. No matter what the situation, once she is in possession of all the facts, good or bad, she will deal with any problem,' says PJ.

'Looking back over the years in politics,' reflects Breda, 'I can't say I did not enjoy them. Life was exciting, never humdrum; our lives were encircled by tensions, and uncertainties.

'I asked PJ on many ocassions if he would leave CJH to go into the private sector, but he would never abandon ship if the going got rough. His plan was to leave the day CJH left, job or no job. But, as things turned out the new Taoiseach, Albert Reynolds asked him to stay on. He was very honoured to be asked but really we both had had enough of politics and he stayed until a replacement was found – Sean Duignan, 'Diggy' as he is affectionately known.

'I admire PJ's loyalty tremendously and he will always be closely identified with the CJH era. He admired and respected Charlie Haughey thoroughly and enjoyed the cut and thrust of politics.

'We will be celebrating our silver wedding anniversary this Autumn and as I reflect over the last 25 years I can only think of the good times which certainly outweigh the bad – I hope the next 25 will be as happy and exciting.'

14

Tears for Old Friends

'They were most unjust... going on this so-called conscience line. This belief that they are somehow different to the rest of us in public life, that they somehow represent integrity and honesty in a way that no other party does, is absolute rubbish. They are just as venal as everyone else when it comes down to it, particularly when it comes to appointments or sharing the spoils of office.'

At exactly 11pm on 11 February 1992, the new Taoiseach, Albert Reynolds, presented his Cabinet to President Mary Robinson at Aras An Uachtarain. It was the first occasion that journalists were allowed to witness the event – previous Presidents had insisted on a photocall only.

Among those who arrived with the fourteen ministers were PJ Mara, and Albert Reynolds' long-time press officer, Bart Cronin.

As PJ walked in, he met the President's personal adviser, Bride Rosney. 'Oh, we see each other across a crowded room every Saturday,' exclaimed PJ, referring to his regular lunches in the Unicorn restaurant on Merrion Row.

While the two had never spoken before, they knew quite a lot about each other.

Bride Rosney, a former School Principal, had become one of Mary Robinson's closest friends and was part of the key team that secured her spectacular election as the Republic's First Citizen.

The last few years had been very difficult, the final six months gruesome. In a sense Mara was glad it was finally at an end.

When the President had finished presenting the seals of office, the Cabinet held its first short meeting, in accordance with tradition, sitting around the same table as the the first Irish Cabinet.

Robinson's election was a real blow for Fianna Fail and Charles Haughey, who had believed they had the ideal candidate in Brian Lenihan.

It was Mara and Charlie McCreevy who had come up with Lenihan's name first, back in the Autumn of 1989 as part of a strategy to ease grassroots' anger at the idea of coalition.

'The rationale was faultless,' wrote Emily O'Reilly in her book *Candidate*.

'Lenihan, the most popular man in Fianna Fail, was the one candidate they were unlikely to turn on if he ran for President. Anger would be put to one side to help "good old Brian" – the grassroots would in turn be boosted by a good election and would then be less likely to knife the party in the back at the local elections.'

However, Haughey remained curiously cool on Lenihan's candidacy, although he had hinted at it at the Cairde Fail dinner that year.

John Wilson also threw his hat in the ring, but Lenihan won the nomination.

Mara explains Haughey's hesitation by pointing to his 'wait and see' attitude to most issues.

'He'd never say anything, but he would always try to make sure that everything was right, and that the organisation was happy with it.

John Wilson made it clear that he wanted to run, and that was that. There was no rancour.'

But there were considerable worries about Brian Lenihan's health. He had undergone a life-saving liver transplant at the Mayo Clinic in the United States, but managed to get elected to the Dail in the 1989 election without personally participating in the campaign.

After Lenihan's nomination, Haughey read out a medical report on his condition to the parliamentary party meeting which stated that he was well fit to take up the position of President. It was suspected, however, that the Taoiseach had left out some of the conditions for his future behaviour.

The *Sunday Tribune* tried desperately to get their hands on a copy of the report, and failed. They printed their efforts on the front page of the edition of 14 November.

Asked if he accepted that the public had a right to know details concerning Mr Lenihan's health, Mara replied: 'The public is entitled to know f*** all about that kind of detail, in my view. That is on the record.' What the *Sunday Tribune* didn't print was that Mara told the reporter that he would furnish them with a copy of Lenihan's medical report, if they would give him one on the editor of the *Sunday Tribune*, Vincent Browne!

The state of Lenihan's health always seemed to touch a nerve with Mara.

Mark O'Connell, then a reporter with the *Irish Press*, once rang him to find out who paid for the entire operation. Mara wasn't in, but soon phoned back.

'The Tanaiste's health is no business of yours,' he snapped.

O'Connell: 'Hold on, there's a story going around that the Government may have paid the cost...'

Mara: 'The Tanaiste's health, as I told you, is none of your f*** business. Do you think I've nothing better to do with my time than to be answering your stupid questions about Brian Lenihan....'

O'Connell: 'It's in the public interest if public money is spent, and...'.

Mara: 'Look, I told you, I've better things to be doing with my time. The Tanaiste's health is none of your business, right?' With that, Mara slammed down the phone!

'I am very fond of Brian Lenihan,' says PJ, 'he is one of my favourite human beings. He has been a friend of mine for 25 years. I felt, at that time, that some of the press treatment of him was ghastly, that some writers who knew him well and should have known better, tried to portray him either as an ogre or as an invalid, depending on the piece. He was, and is, neither. Brian Lenihan is an inspirational figure for all those who have to confront serious illness. He is one of the most civilised people in Irish public life.'

Worried that Fianna Fail was not putting its back into the campaign, a key group of Lenihan supporters, including barrister Esmond Smyth (later appointed a Circuit Court judge), Dr Martin Mansergh and former Government Press Secretary, Frank Dunlop, began preparing scripts on issues of concern. But despite PJ Mara's best attempts to whip up interest in the news desks, the scripts fell largely on deaf ears. Special emphasis was to be placed on the environment and on sport, but nobody took much heed.

'Looking back,' says Mara, 'I think the campaign could have focussed more on Brian Lenihan's record. It should have focussed on Brian as a popular, likeable individual. He did have a significant body of achievements as well as a long service in various departments.

'This is something many people forget about Lenihan. He has a record of significant political achievements in many areas. He was a reforming Justice Minister, an outstanding Fisheries Minister, a tough negotiator in Brussels as Agriculture Minister and a very well respected Foreign Minister. He was a serious, respected, political force within Fianna Fail for thirty years. His only weakness, in my view, is that he is too kind and indulgent to time-wasters.

'Robinson had focussed on her achievements and on what she might do.

'We had too limited a view of the role of the presidency. We were taking a strict constitutional view as laid down by people like Declan Costello and John Kelly. But we should have had a more Childers-like campaign.'

One afternoon early in the presidential election campaign, PJ Mara's phone rang. It was Fianna Fail General Secretary Frank Wall.

Wall alerted Mara to the fact that a young student with Fine Gael leanings, called Jim Duffy, was going about the UCD campus 'boasting' that he had a taped interview with Brian Lenihan in which he claimed to have rung Aras An Uachtarain on the night the FG/Labour coalition collapsed on 27 January 1982. Mara noted the fact.

Then on 16 October at a debate in UCD, Jim Duffy could not believe his ears when he heard Brian Lenihan declare that he had never tried to telephone President Hillery. Word spread, and so erupted the infamous tapes controversy. From then on, Fianna Fail and PJ Mara were engaged in a damage limitation exercise.

When the *Irish Times* ran a front page story by political correspondent, Denis Coghlan, claiming the paper had 'corroborative evidence' that Lenihan had telephoned the Aras, PJ rang the editor, Conor Brady, to point out Duffy's Fine Gael links.

Brady assured Mara their story was solidly based.

'If the case was a criminal one,' said Brady, 'people have gone to the electric chair on less evidence!'

So on Tuesday, 25 October the *Irish Times* did a most unusual thing for a newspaper – they held a press conference to release the relevant portion of the tape.

Student Jim Duffy was accompanied by managing editor, Eoin McVey, and deputy editor, Ken Gray. No questions were taken, and all left immediately. But the effect on the Lenihan camp was devastating.

'One of the things I find weird,' says Mara, ' is that Duffy's connections with Fine Gael were never emphasised by the media, or the fact that the *Irish Times* never allowed any questioning by journalists.

'I know that if I invited journalists to a press briefing and did not allow questions, there would be one hell of a reaction!

'The only other time I remember it being done was by Sean Doherty in his press conference on the telephone tapping affair. It raises serious issues about the standards of journalism and the standards of journalists.'

PJ Mara says he does not know whether or not Brian Lenihan tried to telephone Paddy Hillery.

'I can't remember what happened last week, so how can I remember that exactly? But so what if he did? It would have been a perfectly legitimate thing to do.

'There was total confusion that night. I remember being in the back of the visitors' gallery in the Dail and watching Jim Kemmy turning right instead of left.

'I shouted out: "Oh my God! The Government is gone, Good luck!" And I headed for the fifth floor.'

'But there was a genuinely weird atmosphere about this whole Duffy thing. Brian Lenihan definitely believes he did not ring the Aras.'

Back on the campaign trail Lenihan was canvassing at a shopping centre at Sutton Cross in Dublin. RTE's presenter of *Six One News*, Sean Duignan, got through to Niamh O'Connor on the election bus and asked for an interview with Lenihan. Niamh rang PJ Mara and he agreed.

Before setting off for RTE, Lenihan spoke with Mara on the mobile telephone. But did he advise Lenihan to look directly into the camera, advice that caused Ann Lenihan to say later that whoever gave it should be taken out and shot?

'This whole thing has been blown out of proportion,' claims Mara. 'I told him not to mind Sean Duignan or the political correspondents. I said to him: 'You are speaking to the Irish people and you've got to sound as persuasive as you can.'

Fianna Fail's election campaign was in tatters.

Fine Gael lost little time in putting down a motion of 'no confidence' and the focus of attention was once again on the Progressive Democrats.

Their two Cabinet ministers were in a corner and decided to ask for Lenihan's resignation, although they did not believe it would come. A series of tense meetings followed, with Brian Lenihan refusing to resign. The climax came when Charles Haughey finally sacked his long-time friend from his post as Tanaiste and Minister for Defence.

Two of the men who had strongly supported it in the end were Charlie McCreevy and PJ Mara.

Despite the fact that the three PD ministers had their resignations statements already written, PJ Mara says he is still not too sure what would have happened if they were told to go and jump!

'I knew in my heart Lenihan would have to go, but I was hoping against hope. We discussed it backwards and forwards. People were playing a game, but the Taoiseach had to carry the can. The price was very high. It was all fine and dandy until the TDs would be heading back in their cars to their constituencies, with the envelopes in the boot, saying: 'F***you, Charlie, this is a fine mess!'

But I can understand that Brian Lenihan had to keep his dignity by refusing to resign. But when you came down to the wire, the question was could we have an election in the teeth of Christmas. In the circumstances Fianna Fail stood to lose both the Presidential election and the general election. The party would not blame Brian Lenihan or PJ Mara or anyone else, but one Charles J Haughey! Haughey's action was correct and I supported it, but I was shocked.'

Mara still gets visibly angry at the behaviour of the Progressive Democrats at that time.

'They were most unjust... going on this so-called conscience line. This belief that they are somehow different to the rest of us in public life, that they somehow represent integrity and honesty in a way that no other party does is all absolute rubbish. They are just as venal as everyone else when it comes down to it, particularly when it comes to appointments or sharing the spoils of office.'

After his sacking, Brian Lenihan's campaign began to revive as sympathy poured in for him and Mary Robinson came under intense fire over the abortion issue.

But then Padraig Flynn intervened.

Speaking on an RTE *Saturday View* programme from the Castlebar studio, Flynn accused Mary Robinson of having 'a new interest in family.' Flynn was immediately pounced on by the chairman of the Progressive Democrats, Michael McDowell, who was in the Dublin studio. Outrage followed and Flynn was forced to issue a full apology – he wrote a personal letter to Mary Robinson.

Brenda O'Hanlon, one of the key people in the Robinson camp later claimed that the Flynn episode had cost Lenihan an estimated 80,000 votes.

PJ Mara describes the entire Flynn episode as a 'misinterpretation'.

'Brian was certainly rolling back that weekend and that stopped him...it stopped the bandwaggon. But after the Duffy business the organisation had got behind him in a way that it hadn't before.'

Without the tapes controversy, Mara believes that Lenihan would have 'squeezed in' narrowly, by about the same majority as De Valera beat TF O'Higgins.

'But,' he adds, 'maybe it was that Mary Robinson's time had come. Maybe.'

Evening Herald

15

Answer the Question

*'There's no such thing as a Government secret anymore. The invention
of the photocopier finished that.'*

The first Sunday in September is the major date in the annual hurling
calender, the day of the All-Ireland Final. On 1 September 1991 it was
the turn of Tipperary and Kilkenny.

There was huge interest in the game. Tipperary, long the home of
hurling, had been out in the wilderness for 17 years, until finally they
made a comeback in 1989. Now they were seeking their 24th All-
Ireland title.

Kilkenny were equally determined to win; their last title was back
in 1983 when they had beaten Cork.

Kilkenny were given a further boost by their new manager, the
famous goalkeeper Ollie Walsh.

The 64,000 thousand fans, in their black and amber or blue and
gold, who thronged the streets of Dublin on Sunday morning paid
scant attention to a very complex legal story on the front page of the
Sunday Independent. The story, by journalist Sam Smyth, told of how
the chief executive of the Sugar Company, Chris Comerford, was
suing the directors of a Jersey-based company, Talmino, which had
sold its stake in a subsidiary of the Sugar Company, Irish Sugar
Distributors. Comerford claimed he owned a stake in Talmino.

Few understood the implications of the story, and there was little
follow-up reporting over the next 24 hours.

But the story came like a bombshell to one man as he read it in his
luxury West Cork home. Bernie Cahill, the chairman of the Sugar

Company knew nothing of the deal or the case, and was greatly alarmed. Cahill acted quickly, and within days Chris Comerford had left the company.

The story had major implications for the Government and the Minister for Agriculture, Michael O'Kennedy, whose direct responsibility it was to oversee the Sugar Company.

No one felt the pressure more than PJ Mara, to whose lot it fell to try to put a brave face on events and happenings he again knew nothing about.

Later, Mara would chalk down 1 September as the beginning of the end. It marked the opening of the last and most difficult chapter in his job as Government Press Secretary.

Over the next six months, life would become one long litany of explanations and counter-explanations, leading from crisis to crisis. It was to be the least enjoyable period of his career.

But the seeds of the crisis had already been sown some years before, and involved a multi-million meat baron, Larry Goodman.

The name of Larry Goodman was synonymous with the beef industry, and Goodman's name was closely linked – in the public mind at least – to Charles Haughey.

The link went back primarily to a high-powered press conference in June 1987 when a £260 million plan was launched for Goodman International.

The wide-ranging plan involved building a number of green field plants, as well as upgrading many others.

The Taoiseach, Charles Haughey himself chaired the conference while Agriculture Minister Michael O'Kennedy and his Junior Minister Joe Walsh competed for the highest place at the table.

However, the project never got off the ground. Later, questions would be raised as to how the IDA had given the go-ahead in such a short time, and the role played by a number of key figures, including the Secretary of the Taoiseach's own department.

The media became very interested in Larry Goodman, who adopted a defensive policy of issuing writs. A number of anomalies were uncovered.

In March 1989, it was discovered that the Department of Agriculture had carried out a raid on a Goodman plant in north Dublin.

The month before, Fianna Fail TD Liam Lawlor resigned as chairman of the Oireachtas Committee on State Sponsored Bodies when it emerged that Larry Goodman wanted to buy the State-owned Sugar Company. Lawlor was a director of a Goodman controlled company, Food Industries.

Then speaking with Dail privilege, Labour TD Barry Desmond raised a series of questions in the House about alleged fraudulent practices in Goodman companies. More allegations were made by the Workers Party.

Desmond found more information, including a discovery that a £1 million fine had been imposed on a Goodman company by the Department of Agriculture.

Michael O'Kennedy at first vigorously defended his department in regulating the meat industry, but soon had to admit to irregularities amounting to many millions of pounds.

In April 1988, a series of questions by the PD deputy, Pat O'Malley, uncovered the fact that massive amounts of export credit insurance had been granted to Larry Goodman for trade with Iraq. The insurance had been cancelled by a previous Minister for Industry and Commerce, Michael Noonan.

The PD leader led a campaign in the Dail pointing to the close association between Larry Goodman and Charles Haughey.

'Members of this present government, from the Taoiseach down, are extremely close personally to the leading figure in the group concerned,' he told the Dail in May 1989.

O'Malley claimed that the extraordinarily generous behaviour of the Government towards Goodman virtually excluded everybody else in the meat and other industries. The then Minister for Industry and Commerce, Ray Burke, vigorously rejected the claims.

The general election of 1989 saw Des O'Malley appointed Minister for Industry and Commerce as part of a deal to uncover the full facts of the credit insurance puzzle, and sort them out.

Soon the new minister made the startling revelation that showed the insurance cover given to Larry Goodman for exports to Iraq was greater than the total exports in 1987/88.

However, events were shortly overcome when the entire Goodman organisation nearly collapsed, and special legislation had to be enacted to save the group.

But a television programme on ITV on 13 May brought the Goodman controversy to the top of political agenda again when it revealed new information on the running of the meat plants.

Uproar followed in Leinster House, and attempts by the Government to prevent debate only made matters worse. Haughey was finally forced to give in and a day-long debate followed.

The Progressive Democrats yet again found they had difficulty in supporting Fianna Fail, in the shape of a motion of confidence in the meat industry.

In the end, after more huffing and puffing, Haughey gave in to their request for a judicial tribunal into the entire meat industry. So was born a lengthy and protracted enquiry with just one member, the President of the High Court, Mr Justice Liam Hamilton. The carrying out of the brief involved Mr. Justice Hamilton in referrals to the High Court and Supreme Court in an extensive effort to unravel various complicated webs, both inside and outside Government Buildings.

Politically, the PDs had twice faced down Charles Haughey successfully. They would do so again, until finally they would demand the ultimate – the head of Charles Haughey himself.

The Greencore and Beef Tribunal affairs were further complicated by yet more scandals including one involving the proposed purchase of a new headquarters in Ballsbridge by Telecom Eireann. It was later discovered that the chairman of Telecom, Dr Michael Smurfit, had a share in the company which sold the site to Telecom.

Smurfit resigned from his post, as did Seamus Paircear, the chairman of the company which sold the site, but who also happened to be chairman of the Custom House Docks Development Board.

During all this time PJ Mara's telephone scarcely stopped ringing as media queries poured in, now with added interest from British correspondents.

But PJ was in fighting form.

As the Greencore controversy intensified, Mara accused the Labour party leader, Dick Spring, of being the mouthpiece of Chris Comerford. During his briefing with political correspondents he posed a question about Spring's association with Pat Doherty, a property developer involved in the Telecom controversy.

A report in the *Irish Times* on 9 November 1991 stated that opinion was divided on whether Mara's handling of the Pat Doherty/Dick Spring 'association' was a slip or a confidence trick. It was remarked that PJ uncharacteristically referred to written notes before briefing reporters.

'One correspondent believes that Mara fluffed the throw in uncharacteristic fashion,' continued the report, 'another says that the exercise was a calculated attempt to illustrate the folly of implying guilt by association. In any event, the ploy clearly did not anticipate the wave of outrage it was to provoke in the opposition benches.'

'The whole Greencore controversy had nothing to do with Fianna Fail, or Charles Haughey,' Mara insists.

'Here we had a group of executives of what was a State company. Who were they? Comerford, a Fine Gael supporter with PD leanings in recent times, and Tully a founder member of the PDs. We had no connection with these people, but we got sucked into it.'

Why?

'Because Bernie Cahill, the chairman of the company, and the man who had to sort out all of the mess created by these gents, a man of the highest reputation, was a director of Conor Haughey's mining company. It was Alice and Franz Kafka on a night out in Wonderland! And to add insult to injury Bernie Cahill is not a Fianna Fail supporter. As far as I'm aware, he's a blueshirt!'

Mara suggests that a more open style of Government by Haughey would have eased the pressure.

'There's no such thing as a Government secret in our society anymore. The smallness of our society, our garrulous disposition and the invention of the photocopier finished that. You're better off to be as transparent as possible, mistakes and all. Ninety-nine per cent of the work can be dealt with in an open fashion.

'If, when answering parliamentary questions on the Greencore business, CJH had, at the very beginning as he did in the end, given complete details of the various meetings he had had with Cahill and their purpose, he would have saved himself a lot of grief. If he had got up and said to Spring: "What else do you need to know?" and saturated him with information – he would have had to sit down.

'Governments create a lot of problems for themselves. It need not be like that. Ministers should insist that the drafting of answers to parliamentary questions is as complete and detailed as can be. It would save them grief in the long run. As I've said, there are no secrets anymore, and information will leak in the long run. It would be healthier for our politics if ministers and governments were to dish it out up-front. Some commentators think that this is not done because politicians want to hide things, but mostly this is not true. Parliamentary questions are answered in a particular way because that is the tradition, that is the way we always answered them.

'Enquiries are unnecessary, expensive, too prolonged and inevitably inconclusive. As the chairman of the Tribunal, Mr Justice Liam Hamilton said, if there was a different approach in the Dail and questions were answered properly, there would be no need for enquiries. Why can't they give the information out in the first place anyway? All these enquiries are a waste of energy and resources which could be better applied. Go and answer the question!'

Dick Walsh, Political Editor of the *Irish Times*, agrees:

'Haughey was obsessed with secrecy. His right hand did not know what his left was doing. Mara should have gone and hit him on the head with the teapot instead of giving it to Margaret Thatcher, and told him: "You've got to answer these questions. Tell the truth and be man enough to do it!"'

Mara believes Charlie Haughey's performance at the Beef Tribunal support his views about more open and forthright answering of questions in the Dáil.

He concludes, 'Charlie Haughey's performance at the Beef Tribunal was a tour de force. He was brilliant! His answers were open, frank and informative; they were delivered with a style and sense of humour and irony which was completely convincing.'

16

Bespoke Suits & Vintage Wines

'As someone who probably thinks that a desk is just something for putting your feet on, PJ Mara's office is perpetually on the move, a walking-talking ferment of bonhomie, gadding around Leinster House, the Shelbourne, the media haunts of Merrion Row, or the exalted inner sanctum of U2 concerts.'

Climb the stairs of Dublin's Shelbourne Hotel and turn right on the first floor level. Then walk down the corridor and enter the second room on the left, room 112. This is the Constitution Room, one of the most historic rooms in Dublin where the Free State Constitution was drafted.

It was here on the night of 4 February 1992 that 30 close friends of PJ Mara gathered to mark the end of his five-year term as Government Press Secretary. The evening was hosted by long-time friend, Paul McGuinness and among the attendance were his wife, Breda, and son, John. Also present were some of the most interesting people in Irish political, business and cultural life, journalists and writers – Eamon Dunphy, Sam Smyth, John Waters, Colm Toibin, Mary Holland and Tony Cronin, PR executive Eileen Gleeson, former Justice Minister Ray Burke, barrister Gerry Danaher, accountant to the rock 'n' roll business worldwide, Ossie Kilkenny, Senator Shane Ross, Dermot Desmond and the women from the fifth floor in Leinster House.

No other venue had even been considered. It was in the Shelbourne – or rather the Horse Shoe bar that PJ Mara did most of his socialising. Designed by architect Sam Stephenson, the bar is one of the last places in his empire that Lord Forte has left alone, despite several threats. Plans to refurbish it have met with immediate outbursts of protest from the hotel's clientele, led, in the main, by Dublin businessman Reggie Hastings.

The Horse Shoe has a unique atmosphere and attracts a wide variety of middle-class Dubliners. There, mobile phones are frowned upon – one former head barman, Jimmy Kelly never allowed them at all! In this convivial atmosphere members of the Government, financiers, lawyers and gossip columnists all rub shoulders.

It was a logical meeting point for PJ Mara. His office in Government Buildings was only minutes away, and it was a relatively safe haven where he was sure of avoiding the hassle often experienced in more public hostelries. There Mara could relax and tell non-political friends of the happenings in Leinster House.

There, for example, he would tell of how he had listened to Senator Professor John A Murphy, and a number of others, similarly inclined in Leinster House, discussing historical revisionism and how we might now look at historical events in a new light and with fresh insight. This was around the time Roy Foster's book was published, *Modern Ireland, 1600-1972,* and had attracted a fair amount of controversy. Mara had not been impressed.

'Look here, John,' he exclaimed, 'the next thing these revisionists will be telling us is that all of the people who died in the Famine were suffering from anorexia nervosa!'

With stories like these, PJ Mara earned a reputation as a first-class raconteur.

It was while chatting to friends one evening in the early eighties that PJ was 'reintroduced' to Eamon Dunphy.

Dunphy had left Dublin in 1960 to take up a football career in England, and only returned to live there again in 1977.

'I had read an article by this PJ Mara in the *Sunday Tribune,* but never connected him with the old PJ Mara of Drumcondra,' he recalls. 'We had completely lost touch.'

The Horse Shoe bar was, at that time a pleasant, quiet place for Eamon Dunphy to come and have a drink.

'There were very few people there, and a very good staff. Jimmy Kelly, the head barman did not tolerate raucous conduct from anyone, be they Government Press Secretary, Oscar-winning producer or whoever.'

But soon the gossip columnists were writing about who was to be seen, or not to be seen, in the Horse Shoe, and it filled up.

'All kinds of chancers started to come in,' says Dunphy.

One evening Mara, Dunphy and Noel Pearson arrived in for a drink only to find there was no seat available. Suddenly Mara turned to his two chums and grinned: 'I feel like I'm in the Zoological Gardens when I come in here now. All these yuppies are coming in here is just to look at us!'

In the Horse Shoe, and other local venues, PJ gathered round him an odd mix of friends from across a wide perspective. Political boundaries were of no consequence.

The chairman of the Progressive Democrats, Michael McDowell – long time the *bête noire* of Charles Haughey – became one of his closest friends, as did fellow senior counsel and PD activist, Adrian Hardiman.

'PJ is a very intelligent fellow,' says Michael McDowell. 'He marries a sense of humour and a pleasant personality very well.

'One of his great attributes is that he punctures pomposity. Nobody could be pompous in his presence. People who got moralistic always found themselves uncomfortable in his company. Crusading journalists like the Kerrigans and the Fintan O'Tooles would find it almost impossible to keep their guard up with PJ because he would just prick them immediately. To someone who felt politics very emotionally he would just say: "Would you ever....." and completely deflate them.'

In the Autumn of 1991 McDowell called in a favour from PJ. He was running a fundraising event for the PDs in his Dublin South constituency. One of the raffle prizes for the evening was a copy of the controversial book *The Boss* by Joe Joyce and Peter Murtagh. McDowell asked PJ to autograph a copy. Relations between the two Government parties were not good at the time.

PJ duly signed his name, and then added wryly: 'I'm quite shameless. I would do almost anything to keep this Government in office!' At the raffle Adrian Hardiman bought the book for £100.

Hardiman and McDowell are two regulars in the Unicorn restaurant on Merrion Row every Saturday where PJ and his wife Breda are also regular attenders.

Run by Miss Dom, the Unicorn, though purely functional, has great charm and is similar to an Italian diner one might find in Milan. It attracts an extraordinary mix of people for Saturday lunch, all with one thing in common – the food is of very secondary importance!

Only two tables are ever reserved – the centre ones for PJ Mara and friends. PJ likes to dine on pasta, and Miss Dom prepares a special oil for him. The Unicorn wine cellar is not vast, but it is pleasant.

But PJ's socialising is now very tame compared to the hell-raising days of the early 1980s when the day was regularly capped with a high-spirited visit to a night club. In tow, on a regular basis, were Senators Shane Ross and Maurice Manning. (Through PJ, Ross was later to introduce Charles Haughey to stock-broker Dermot Desmond).

'We hit it off well,' recalls Shane Ross. 'We were both rather irresponsible and drank far too much.'

Ross remembers the first time they met.

'I met this charming man in the Dail bar and chatted to him for a while. I didn't know who he was but he bought me a drink. Later I asked friends who he was. When I heard the answer I went "Aaagh....." I had this horrific image of this hatchet man of Haughey's who really did the dirty work in the underworld.'

Ross and Mara had a fair amount of free time and were not tied down.

'We spent days in the bar in Leinster House, in Scruffy's and in the Shelbourne Bar. God knows who paid for it all!' Maurice Manning's marriage had broken up and he had 'cut loose' a bit.

'I think Shane Ross is right,' says PJ. 'We did drink more than was good for us. Fianna Fail had just gone into opposition and the hard pounding and long hours of the mid-1980s had not yet commenced. In our own minds we were "things of beauty and boys forever!"'

'PJ is very gentle and courteous and women love him;' says Manning, ' he has a good streak in him and he loves gossip.'

The 1980s bred a great feeling of boom. It was part of the culture to dabble in shares. The boom was largely attributed to the rise in oil shares at the same time.

'There was a euphoric and unreal atmosphere about, which combined with a highly exciting time in politics,' recalls Shane Ross. 'I was an Independent Senator and PJ was a pretty free spirit. We were wild, there is no doubt about that. It was summer madness!'

After a bad night session when the two would not return home until well into the morning of the following day, contact would be made later as to what excuses were offered.

'What excuse did you use this time?' one would anxiously enquire of the other. 'How long was it before SHE spoke to you?'

'Breda Mara is a formidable lady and she has a very effective style for expressing disapproval of bad behaviour,' says PJ.

Then in 1985 Ross and Mara had a bet in the Dail bar as to who would stay off drink the longer. Seven years later Ross is still abstemious. Today Ross and Mara are still close friends, but don't meet as often. Shane Ross felt a little guilty when he did not forewarn PJ that he was joining Fine Gael. But PJ forgave him, although still manages the occasional dig.

One morning recently he rang Ross' home looking for him.

'He's not here,' said his wife, Ruth Buchanan. 'I'm afraid you're out of luck.'

'Oh,' said PJ, 'I forgot the Wicklow County Council Sheep-Dipping Committee meets on a Monday!'

With political contacts came a new sense of elegance, as PJ Mara acquired a taste for the finer things in life.

Today Mara is always impeccably groomed from head to toe.

RTE journalist Michael O'Sullivan remembers first seeing him during the Irish EC Presidency in Dublin Castle in 1990.

'It was an extraordinary sight because he was standing shoulder high above a group of journalists. The thing that struck me was how well dressed he was. He looked straight out of Saville Row. Not only did he stand out from a group of under-dressed Irish hacks, but he stood out in the whole well-dressed circus of a European summit.'

Soon O'Sullivan started to see Mara everywhere.

'I regularly saw him in the Horse Shoe bar in the Shelbourne where he often held court. There he would dispense the most extraordinary hospitality. His generosity came from the heart.'

Shortly after, the elegantly turned-out O'Sullivan himself discovered that he shared the same distinguished bespoke tailor with PJ, Maurice Abrahams of South Anne St. PJ has had his suits hand-made there since 1975.

'I always noted PJ had a fine flannel suit,' says O'Sullivan. 'It's always a sign that somebody knows about tailoring, and about cloth. He always had his suits double-breasted and cut in an absolute classical Saville Row manner.'

'If the begrudgers in Dublin society would have reservations about PJ Mara being a gentleman, I would have none because I believe him to be everything a gentleman should be,' declares the former Vienna-based correspondent of the London *Independent*.

Gentleman that he was, PJ was proposed for membership in 1988 of the highly exclusive Kildare St and University Club on Stephen's Green.

Founded by William Burton Conygham – an ancestor of the present Lord Henry Mountcharles – in 1782, the club was until modern times a bastion of British imperialism equalled only by Dublin Castle. During the last World War the notoriously anti-Irish US Ambassador, David Gray held court regularly in the Kildare St Club and used it as a sounding board for Irish opinion. The cock-eyed reports that he kept sending back to Washington caused no end of trouble for the Taoiseach of the day, Eamon De Valera.

Formerly an exclusively Protestant institution – Daniel O'Connell was 'blackballed' from membership and went and founded the near-by Stephen's Green Club – it has opened its doors on a limited basis to Catholics in recent years.

The club still has a very old-world atmosphere. On arrival at the entrance, you surrender your brief-case and mobile phone – which are strictly forbidden – to the hall porter. Women have only recently been admitted to the dining room for lunch, but are allowed to drink in the bar, for one hour before dinner on two evenings of the week.

The application process for membership is complex. The applicant has to have a proposer, seconder and three 'supporters'.

PJ Mara was proposed by his old friend Shane Ross and seconded by solicitor Alan Graham. His 'supporters' were Adrian Hardiman, former FG minister George Birmingham, and Michael McDowell.

But Mara's application did raise a few hackles in the thick cigar smoke over after-dinner port. 'Will this Mara chap be bringing a lot of tabloid Johnnies in here?' demanded one member.

When his application eventually came up before the club election committee for ratification, one strongly Anglo-Irish accent popped up from behind.

'I see this Mr Mara is the Government Press Secretary,' said RB McDowell, Emeritus Professor of History at Trinity College. 'But which government?'

'And something else, Ross,' warned another. 'I hope that when I come into lunch in future now that this chap Mara is a member, that I won't find bloody Ghadaffi in the Members' dining room!'

However, despite the doubts, PJ Mara was elected to membership. He took to it like a duck to water.

He would frequently dine there, often alone, and never at the members' table. He once told a friend that the reason he joined the club was because his friends were members. He didn't join the nearby Stephen's Green Club because he didn't know many there. However, Charles Haughey had once been a member but allowed his name to lapse in recent years. It was never renewed.

'When dining, PJ likes to eat well,' says one member.

Writing in his Dubliner's Diary column in the *Evening Press* in August 1988, Michael O'Toole wrote: 'The important thing about PJ's prospective membership of the Kildare St and University Club is the blow that will be struck to the Horse Shoe bar of the Shelbourne. Poor Lord Forte won't know what has hit him, and Jimmy Kelly (the head barman) will probably go into mourning.'

One of Mara's great abilities was to be at home in any company.

In his job he was subjected to a lot of boring people, but showed great patience with them, much more so than Haughey.

'He can negotiate his way around a French menu, or a wine list as well as being able to wolf down the old Chicken Maryland like a trooper,' says journalist Declan Lynch. He continues: 'As someone who probably thinks that a desk is just something for putting your feet on, PJ's office is perpetually on the move, a walking-talking ferment of *bonhomie*, gadding around Leinster House, the Shelbourne, the media haunts of Merrion Row, or the exalted inner sanctum of U2 concerts.'

Mara has been to several U2 concerts, and enjoyed all of them. His closeness to the band arises from his friendship with manager Paul McGuinness.

McGuinness got to know Mara in 1985 when a company with which he is closely associated, Windmill Lane, took over the Fianna Fail party political broadcasts. They also shared mutual friends Shane Ross and Noel Pearson.

'He seemed to look on politics almost as a sport,' says Paul McGuinness. 'I went to the Fianna Fail Ard Fheis a few times. We used to say that PJ comes to my gigs and I go to his!'

McGuinness was very struck by how knowledgeable Mara was, and how very well read.

A great interest of Mara's was the former American President, Lyndon B Johnson. When in Texas – which has everything that does not move named after LBJ – McGuinness collected all the memorabilia he could find, and brought them back to Mara.

In turn, Mara presented McGuinness with a book on Johnson with the inscription: 'If LBJ had been born in Ireland, he would have been in Fianna Fail!' At least they had similar election machines.

Holidaying in Antibes after the 1989 general election, McGuinness was again surprised to find Mara sitting under a sunshade reading the poems of English poet, Philip Larkin.

McGuinness was always amazed at Mara's charisma and his almost magnetic ability to attract people.

Once in New York during a party fund-raising tour, McGuinness was organising the after-dinner entertainment.

'I knew an eaterie, the Columbus, which is owned by actor Robert De Niro and others. I reserved places for ten, thinking it would be enough. But suddenly dozens of people started to arrive, all in dinner jackets, sent with the encouragement of Mara. Eventually the management threw everybody who was not wearing a dinner jacket out of the restaurant ! So we had the whole place to ourselves.'

McGuinness is very impressed with Mara's media skills, and it is likely the two will form a closer working relationship in the years ahead.

PJ and Breda have a permanent invite to join U2 when on tour.

17

Give us Barabbas!

'I never assassinated anyone's character, nor bad-mouthed anyone in a vicious or damaging way.'

Journalist Sam Smyth had an appointment with PJ Mara in the Horse Shoe bar in the Shelbourne Hotel. It was the early Spring of 1992 and Smyth had been away in the United States.

While he was missing, there had been some extraordinary political developments.

Former Justice Minister Sean Doherty had held a press conference at which he stated that he had handed all the transcripts of the taped telephone conversations of journalists Geraldine Kennedy and Bruce Arnold in 1982 to the then Taoiseach, Charles Haughey.

Haughey reacted immediately, vigorously denying the allegations. However, an opinion poll showed that the people believed Doherty. Haughey had decided to resign in order to avoid a general election.

'It was unsustainable, P.,' said Sam, 'Three out of four believed Doherty.' Mara sighed and said: 'No Sam, it was the Irish people saying: "Give us Barabbas!"'

It had been an eventful six months. By the late summer of 1991, it had become apparent that yet another heave was starting to swell up against Charles Haughey within his own parliamentary party.

'There was a period in September 1991,' says Mara 'when some people were getting restless. It was nothing you could put your finger on, but it was around.'

Throughout the Autumn, a group known as the Country and Western Alliance emerged. With Albert Reynolds as the focus, this group comprised Environment Minister Padraig Flynn and junior ministers Maire Geoghegan-Quinn, Noel Treacy and Michael Smith. There were frequent reports of sightings of Padraig Flynn visiting Albert Reynolds' luxury apartment in Ballsbridge.

Another key to any move was Bertie Ahern, who, however, remained totally loyal to Haughey. Ahern had promised to support Reynolds whenever Haughey stood down and publicly said that he, himself was not yet ready for the top job. But as Finance Minister under Haughey, he would be the automatic choice when Reynolds retired. This 'dream ticket' of Reynolds and Ahern was seen to unite the urban and rural strands of Fianna Fail in a new and dynamic way.

When the Cabinet reconvened after the summer recess, Reynolds went on the offensive by hinting that the full terms of the recently negotiated Programme for Economic and Social Progress (PESP) might not be met if the budget strategy was to be adhered to.

An interview on RTE's *This Week* programme reiterating the same view, drew the sharp response from PJ Mara that this was 'typical Department of Finance rhetoric.'

'Albert's comments really annoyed Haughey,' says Mara, 'and the other members of the Government.'

'There were worries that the pay level for the public service was high, but written into the PESP was a clause which provided that any problems arising in any area such as public sector pay would be dealt with through the Central Review Committee of the PESP. Any public comment about inability to pay was wrong, because it put the trade union leadership under immense pressure. There was a substantial body of opinion within the trade union movement that did not approve of these deals anyway, and the view was taken by Haughey and the Government that any public comments were injudicious, to say the least.'

Mara was told by Haughey to defend the agreement. 'I was given instructions that this was to be dealt with in a clear and unambiguous manner and that's what happened. It was not an attempt to undermine anybody, but simply to express the view of the Government that any public comments were unwise. A very serious view was taken of such comments by the trade union movement, and indeed by all the social partners.'

But fate was against Haughey.

The Greencore scandal broke, and although Haughey was not to blame, he suffered badly from the fall-out.

Rather than help to ease worries, Haughey positively alarmed many back-bench deputies when he jokingly commented on RTE radio that 'some of these Chinese leaders go on 'till they are 80 or 90, but I think that's probably a bit long!'

Meanwhile four deputies who had been on holiday together in Cyprus – MJ Nolan, Noel Dempsey, Liam Fitzgerald and Sean Power – decided to increase the pressure by issuing a statement expressing their disquiet over the handling of recent events.

At a subsequent parliamentary party meeting, two of them – Power and Dempsey – told Haughey he should go.

Haughey didn't go, but went on to narrowly survive a 'no confidence' motion in the Dail in an eleventh hour deal with the PDs on a renewed Programme for Government. Here, the intervention of Bertie Ahern had saved the day.

But rumours of a new revolt among the back-benchers continued until finally, on 6 November, Sean Power decided to put down a motion following a very unsatisfactory meeting of the parliamentary party. The motion placed Reynolds and the other disgruntled ministers in a dilemma.

First to decide was Reynolds, who let it be known that he would support Power's motion. However, he refused to resign as Minister for Finance and Haughey promptly fired him.

Padraig Flynn followed Reynolds within 24 hours and was also fired. Junior ministers Maire Geoghegan-Quinn, Noel Treacy and

Michael Smith also indicated support for the motion, but they were not fired as it required a decision of Cabinet, rather than of the Taoiseach.

As the morning of the vote approached, tension reached record levels within Fianna Fail. This was illustrated most poignantly by the Minister for Foreign Affairs, Gerry Collins, who appeared on TV and accused Albert Reynolds of showing 'appalling immaturity'.

The meeting on Saturday, 9 November — again held in the infamous fifth floor party rooms in Leinster House — lasted 14 ½ hours.

In his speech Albert Reynolds claimed that he had been the victim of a campaign of misinformation. He blamed the Government Press Secretary, PJ Mara for this, and also surprised those present when he spoke of a white Hiace van being spotted acting suspiciously near his Ballsbridge apartment.

The general view of the meeting was that Reynolds had gone over the top in his complaints, and it became glaringly obvious that Haughey would win the vote. When the roll was finally called at 2am on Sunday, the result was 55 votes to 22.

When the allegations of misinformation were made during the meeting, it was decided that a Commission would be established to investigate them, comprising of party chairman, Jim Tunney, Albert Reynolds and John Wilson.

PJ Mara is dismissive of the entire episode.

'My only comment is that nobody ever spoke to me except Jim Tunney, who mentioned it very briefly. The whole thing about Hiace vans and a campaign of misinformation was absolute and total rubbish.'

However, while there may be no evidence of any Hiace van, Emily O'Reilly, political correspondent of the *Irish Press* claims there were moves to discredit Reynolds, and PJ had certainly played a role.

'There was an attempt to link Albert with non-political people and show him in a bad light.'

The chairman of the Progressive Democrats, Michael McDowell, describes the Hiace van episode as 'a nonsense'.

'But,' he adds, 'PJ had a healthy contempt for Albert at the time. His view was that Reynolds was not half as capable as Haughey.

Mara insists that at all times his job was to defend Charlie Haughey and the Government.

On one occasion, when this writer asked PJ about reports that Reynolds was in fact taking soundings for the leadership, he replied:

'Albert's running a few flags up the flagpole to see if anybody will salute!'

Later, when Mara worked briefly as Government Press Secretary for Albert Reynolds, he claimed to have shown the same response when urging the Taoiseach to take a tough line with Senator Des Hanafin and the Pro-Life groups.

One of Mara's methods of operations was to push a story to reporters. Mark O'Connell of the *Sunday Business Post* recalls him quietly mentioning names like Liam Lawlor and John Ellis as being involved in an anti-Haughey plot. This tactic would force others to immediately publicly disassociate themselves from the move.

'These people were frozen out, and the potential leaders ran for cover,' adds O'Connell.

But despite Haughey's win, Albert Reynolds' claims against PJ Mara led to a barrage of questions to Haughey at official Dail Question Time on the following Wednesday, 13 November.

Fine Gael's Alan Shatter was first off, demanding that the Taoiseach outline the specific functions of the Government Press Secretary.

Mr Haughey gave the following reply:

'The Government Press Secretary is required under his contract of employment to perform the duties appropriate to his position.

'As has been the case with his predecessors in the past, his work in practice consists principally of ensuring that the media are kept informed of Government decisions and policies, and of securing from Ministers and Departments, information sought by the media in respect of the activities of these Ministers and Departments.'

Having established that the holder of the office was a Civil Servant, Deputy Shatter asked how it could be that an internal Fianna Fail party committee was going to investigate this particular 'Civil Servant's' conduct?

Taoiseach: 'There is not any committee. Our party for their own good reasons decided to carry out an enquiry. It has nothing to do with Government or with the Civil Service. It is a party matter.'

Fine Gael leader John Bruton asked the Taoiseach if the Government Press Secretary was required to abstain from party political activity as a Civil Servant?

Taoiseach: 'The position of the Government Press Secretary is traditionally a very in-between area. It would be ridiculous to think of him as a Civil Servant in the normal terms of a Civil Servant, or as being bound by the normal procedures which generally apply to Civil Servants. Traditionally, the Government Press Secretary is very much a political person. He comes and goes with his political masters and it is quite absurd to suggest that he is totally divorced from the political realities of his position.'

The House erupted in shouts from the Opposition when Mr Haughey insisted that the Government Press Secretary was entitled to engage in political activity. Workers Party deputy Pat Rabbitte asked the Taoiseach if it was an abuse 'of the current occupant's talents' that he should be used as 'some kind of personal streetwise Jeeves to the Taoiseach' and that it was an abuse for him to spread disinformation about members of the House.

The questions concluded with Alan Shatter declaring that the Taoiseach's failure to answer the questions adequately 'confirms that what was said last week about the former Minister for Finance was at the behest of the Taoiseach'.

In an interview with the *Sunday Tribune* on 22 December, PJ Mara was asked about John Bruton's description of him as a 'character assassin'.

'I never assassinated anyone's character, nor bad-mouthed anyone in a vicious or damaging way,' he replied. 'I told as many stories against myself as I told about people like John Bruton.'

Back in Leinster House in November 1991, Charles Haughey was to astound his supporters and critics alike, when he appointed two backbench TDs, Noel Davern and Dr Jim McDaid as his Cabinet replacements for the deposed ministers.

The two men were very popular within the rank and file of the party, but junior ministers and other back-benchers like Dick Roche, who had to carry the can for the party time and again, felt badly let down.

'A bombshell hit the Dail when the leader of the Workers Party, Proinsias De Rossa told the House that McDaid had been photographed with a leading IRA man, James Pius Clarke, on the steps of the Four Courts during the hearing of his extradition case. McDaid had, at all times, made it clear that he supported Government policy on extradition.

However, the appointment seemed particularly insensitive. The PDs reviewed the matter but McDaid pre-empted any coalition crisis by withdrawing his nomination publicly in the Dail. He had been Minister for Defence for just half a day.

The Government was saved, but Haughey's political judgement was firmly back under the microscope.

PJ Mara agrees that the appointments were a mistake.

'Both of them, who are very good friends of mine, would have been happy to be appointed as junior ministers. In my view it was no time to be experimenting. Haughey should have done what he did all his life, and looked at the percentage game. He should have promoted people like Joe Walsh in Cork and Frank Fahey in Galway.

'He would then have had two new able ministers and five junior posts to give away. Bring in Davern, McDaid and three others, strategically placed, and everyone would have been happy. The whole revolt was over. These people had gambled and lost. But Haughey weakened his position by making these appointments.'

Then came Doherty's bazooka!

Back in the Fianna Fail fold, Sean Doherty had been quietly working his way back up the Fianna Fail ladder.

Having failed to win either a European Parliament seat or a Dail seat in the general election of 1989, he had been very lucky when his name came out of the hat in a tied vote for the Cathaoirleach of the Seanad. The job carried a salary of £28,894, expenses and a State car.

But deep in his heart Doherty's ambition was to get back to the Dail, and ministerial office. While Cathaoirleach of the Seanad he once told Haughey he was only there to 'get back the seat that was out on hire-purchase to Tom Foxe in Roscommon!'

But underneath it all Doherty had been seething over the fact that he had been made to carry the can, as he thought, over the tapping of two journalists' telephones back in 1982.

His anger erupted when the Minister for Justice, Ray Burke, published the Interception of Postal Packets and Telecommunications Messages (Regulation) Bill 1992, in early December of 1991, as part of the agreed Programme for Government.

On a *Nighthawks* programme on RTE he dropped a major surprise when he said that he felt let down by the fact that 'other people knew what he was doing.'

Then, on 21 January following a visit to Spain, Doherty called a press conference in the Montrose Hotel in Dublin – he wanted to be near RTE due to a journalists' strike and the difficulties in getting coverage.

'I am confirming tonight that the Taoiseach, Mr Haughey was fully aware in 1982 that two journalists' phones were being tapped, and that he at no stage expressed a reservation about his action.'

According to Doherty he had taken the transcripts of the tapes, given them to Mr Haughey personally and left them in his possession.

'At no stage did he indicate disapproval of the action which had been taken,' he added.

He announced he would be resigning as Cathaoirleach and left the hotel room without answering a single question. He could not be contacted for weeks.

The PDs held an emergency meeting, and agreed they could no longer support Haughey in government.

Haughey fought back, bravely, at a press conference where he denied all Doherty's claims. He went on to answer questions for over an hour.

But it was too late, and on Wednesday night, 22 January, Charles J Haughey decided to relinquish the post of Taoiseach and leader of Fianna Fail after twelve years.

PJ Mara is still bitter about Sean Doherty.

A man, who does not normally harbour a grudge, Mara sits up and speaks disdainfully when the subject of Sean Doherty is raised.

Ironically the two had been great friends.

Back in the early 1980s when he was Minister for Justice, he often stayed with the Maras at their home in Clontarf. They also mixed a lot together socially.

PJ Mara does not believe a word of what Sean Doherty said in the Montrose Hotel. It is, he says, 'in total conflict with what he told me over dinner in February, 1983.'

'We talked about it over a meal in February 1983 when the whole thing was fresh in his memory, and there was nothing at stake. We were out of government, Fianna Fail had lost office, so we were all in the same boat. On the particular evening we discussed it, I remember very clearly saying to him: 'What the f*** were you guys up to?' And I also enquired if Haughey knew about it.

Doherty replied: 'On my oath, Haughey knew nothing whatever about the tappings.'

The first time it was raised, he said, was at a farewell dinner for the Government in Johnny Opperman's restaurant in Malahide in December.

'A story had been written in the *Irish Times* by Peter Murtagh, and Haughey asked Doherty about it. Doherty assured Haughey there was nothing in it, and nothing to worry about. I have since checked that version of the story with a number of members of the Government of that time. They have confirmed to me that Sean Doherty's story of 1983 is the correct one.'

Sean Doherty and PJ Mara have only had two conversations since that time, and both were 'very short'.

18

Scrap Saturday

> *Haughey:*   *Oh, of course, give it to the O'Connors. Have it fixed somehow.*
> *Mara:*   *Yes, Boss. But which O'Connor – Pat?*
> *Haughey:*   *No, give it to the other O'Connor – Pat!'*

Comic, Dermot Morgan never met Charles Haughey. But as a stand-up comedian he had drawn on Mr Haughey's character for material over many years.

'I'm sure he would be very interesting company,' says Morgan. 'But he certainly came across many times as a hardy boyo. But you suspected there was a bit of graciousness in there somewhere as well.'

In the late 1980s Morgan had built up a reputation as a great mimic artist. His appearances on the *Late Late Show* dressed as a Dublin 4 business exec. about to attend a rugby match, brought the country to its knees on Saturday nights.

He set up his own company, Cue Productions, and started a pioneering business in the unstable world of entertainment. He would watch for opportunities which he felt, if properly treated, would catch the public imagination.

He identified one such possibility as the resurgence of the Tipperary hurling team. The premier county had produced some of the great players of the 1960s who displayed their skills in some of the finest matches in the history of the game.

Men like Jimmy and John Doyle, Theo English, and Michael 'Babs' Keating had been the heroes of many teenagers growing up at the time.

Munster hurling finals, particularly those between Tipp. and Cork, had often produced outstanding games of the year.

Writing in the *Sunday Press*, hurling coach Cyril Farrell said: 'Those of us outside the so-called golden vale of Munster hurling have had to endure tales of Cork-Tipperary heroics for years. And yes, they have produced some outstanding clashes, but there were many years when the glamour of the occasion tended to make the quality of hurling look far higher than it actually was.

'As the years pass, tales of previous Cork-Tipperary games form a folklore of which Fionn MacCumhaill would be proud. Strong men standing hip-to-hip, struggling for supremacy with hurleys swishing manfully through the air. And never an ugly stroke pulled!'

'Tipp.,' says Morgan, 'are the Manchester United of hurling. If they're going well, then the championship is always interesting. But without them, it's like the League without Liverpool.'

The son of a Thurles man, Morgan had a special affinity with the Tipperary team, and was overjoyed when the team won the All-Ireland in 1989 after 17 years in the wilderness.

He decided the team was ripe for a documentary to be entitled 'Tipp, Tipp, Hurrah!' So, on 6 June 1992 he sent a film crew, under producer Billy McGrath, to film the first round of the championship between Tipp. and Cork in Pairc Uí Chaoimh. They would interview Babs Keating and a few of the players. But Tipp. were beaten, and Morgan had to shelve his plan!

His plans for a satirical radio series in 1990 were based on less chancy circumstances. His first title for a series was 'Angelus Rehearsal', but RTE quickly knocked that. Finally, ten minutes before he was due to submit his plan, he came up with a title. He thought of the children's programme, 'Scratch Saturday,' and suddenly the name 'Scrap Saturday' hit him.

He submitted his plan, and a pilot programme, to the Director of Radio Programmes, Kevin Healy and producer John P. Kelly. The first series went out in the Autumn of 1990. It consisted of ten 'commercial half hours' (twenty-eight minutes), to which the critics reacted favourably.

The menu for the sketches was as up-to-date as possible. Script writers Morgan and Gerry Stembridge would wait until Thursday night before polishing off the texts for recording on Friday.

The cast, apart from themselves, were actors Owen Roe and Pauline McGlynn...'That,' says Morgan 'is capital 'G,' then L.Y.N.N... I get the head eaten off me if I don't remember that!'

Although only making the occasional appearance in the earlier series, the 'Boss' and his sidekick, 'Maaara', gradually became a weekly item:

Haughey: Mara, this ad in the *Irish Times* jobseeker: 'Executive with press management skills seeks appointment. Pleasant disposition, can take pressure, used to dealing with awkward customers.' I wonder who that might be?

Mara: No idea, Boss.

H: It's you, Mara, thinking the end is nigh.

M: It's just the wife and kid. I have to earn a crust somehow.

H: Keep this nonsense up, Mara, and you will be qualified to be the manager in Ringsend sewage treatment station. And I can give you more shit than the whole of Dublin.

M: Yes, Boss.

H: Stop sobbing. Here, wipe your eyes with this...it's another of those Programmes for National Recovery. Be rational man, who do you think can challenge me?

M: Albert, I suppose, has the troops with him.

H: Self-made man. A fortune indeed. No mystery about making a fortune from grinding up knackered horses to keep Rover's coat shiny. The punters can see the trick, they can see what's up his sleeve, how he made his fortune. They could never fathom how I made mine. That is why I have an air of mystery, charisma. But I will make pet food of Albert. New Pal or should that be Old Chum with added liver, lily-liver and strong hint of chicken!

The programme caught the popular imagination, and made PJ Mara a household name.

While most people knew of his existence, they knew little of him as he never appeared on radio or TV. Haughey did not like being upstaged, and certainly not by his Press Secretary. Mara should neither be seen nor heard, that was the understanding. During all his years as Press Secretary for Fianna Fail, and later as Government Press Secretary, he never gave a single interview to either radio or television.

He, nevertheless delighted in his new caricature. A man who specialised in mimicry himself, he was delighted to sit back on Saturday mornings and listen to his *alter ego*, Maaara.

'I think it was terrific radio because everybody had their own mental picture of the scene in Government Buildings with this fiendish Taoiseach and his slobbering Press Secretary up to all kinds of madness. If that makes people happy in bed on a Saturday morning, so be it.

'It depended very much on good script-writing. When it was right, it was very, very funny, but when it was bad, it was bloody awful!'

Morgan and Stembride deliberately inserted little known details into the sketches. They gave them an air of reality.

'We threw in the fact that the President's escort was the eleventh cavalry squadron. Not many would know that, but it did give it an edge of reality,' says Morgan.

In the second series in 1991, the sacking of Albert Reynolds and the imminent leadership contest were a regular feature:

Mara: Boss, where do we stand? How are we fixed? Have you done a head count?

Haughey: What are you on about, Mara, always fuss and bluster. Have you no time to consider the beauty of life, the passing of the seasons?

M: Yes, but Boss...

H: Consider the lilies of the fields, are they not...?

M: Consider that hure, Reynolds!

H: PJ, you fret so. Come look at the leaves on the trees, see them turning. Autumn, season of mists and mellow fruitfulness. Hear the rustling of the leaves, PJ.

M: Hear the sharpening of the knives.

H: There are no knives being sharpened, Mara. It's all the stress.

M: But Boss, there are murmurings...

H: Of course, there are murmurings of approval. I have delivered the programme for government.

M: Well now Boss, you have to give Bertie some credit.

H: Ah, Bertie. Great little gurrier. Bertie, salt of the earth. Reminds me of myself before I made my first million. Smashing kid. One day, Mara, one day you mark my words, young Bertie will sit where I now sit. I am going to see he is my successor.

M: But he says he needs more experience.

H: Oh, he'll have plenty of that by then.

M: But Boss, tempus fugit. Are you sure Bertie will be ready in the time that's left?

H: For God's sake, Mara, he'll be a great Taoiseach. He will only be 60 then!

For those who knew the real PJ Mara, the voice of the caricature bore no resemblance whatever to the real thing. This was a deliberate ploy.

The part of 'Maaara' was acted by a young Dublin man, Owen Roe. He had trained at the Oscar School and the Brendan Smith Academy.

Roe had starred as George Blake in *Burke and Blake* in the Focus theatre, and in *Murder in the Cathedral* in Christ Church in 1991. He played leading roles in three of Dermot Bolger's plays, and was nominated for best actor award for the part of Eddie Keogh in *One Last White Horse* at the Peacock, one of Bolger's most controversial plays which dealt with the drugs scene.

In the *Scrap Saturday* series he also played the roles of other characters like Derek Davis, Donnchadh O Dulaing, David Hanly and Bertie Rubble.

When it came to choosing a voice for PJ Mara, Morgan and Owen Roe decided that as the public did not know how he sounded, they would invent a voice for him. The tone they decided on was a snappy, slightly Dublin accent which betrayed a blustering, confused Maaara, as he might have been, following Dail allegations that Haughey had misled the House over his meetings with Bernie Cahill in the Greencore affair.

Mara: Here is the cup of tea you asked for, Boss.
Haughey: Cup of tea?
M: Yeah, you asked me to get you a cup of tea.
H: For God's sake Mara, I never...
M: I wrote it down, Boss, 'one cup of tea and a choccie bikkie.'
H: I never attempted to mislead you on the issue of a cup of tea. It is true that I started to say 'cup of tea', but I was interrupted in mid-sentence. Had I not been, I would have told you that what I wanted was such a cup of tea as has no choccie bikkie with it.
M: It's alright, Boss, you don't have to tell me all that.
H: Now what have we got on Spring?
M: Eh, nothing as such ...just at the moment. Eh...I mean...

H: Mara get something on him, or I'll have something on you!

M: What's that, Boss?

H: Oh, just a little piece of paper with something written on it concerning you.

M: Ah, go on Boss. What's the bit of paper, what does it say about me?

H: It gives your gross annual salary, deductions, tax allowances, etc.

M: Eh...?

H: Your P45, Mara, P45!

It is unlikely that Charles Haughey ever listened to *Scrap Saturday*, or if he did, he never discussed it with anybody, and certainly never with PJ Mara.

Haughey rarely listened to radio at all, except while travelling in his car. His interest in television was also limited, and rarely extended much beyond news bulletins.

PJ Mara, on the other hand, monitored as many current affairs programmes as possible throughout the day, beginning with *Morning Ireland.*

However, the *Scrap Saturday* series had been running for a few weeks before he tuned in, as Saturday was a day of relaxation.

'Up to then, RTE comedy series were never in my view very funny, and it was only when someone told me I was in this one myself that Breda and I tuned in. The thing caught the public imagination, and from then on every bloody pub I went into fellows were going 'Maaara, Maaara!' Our son, John, who was in boarding school in Newbridge College, also got a terrible time, with everyone in the school now calling him 'Maaara', instead of by his Christian name!

'But much of the series was absolutely brilliant. I think we need a lot more of its type, or a development of it, as a kind of alternative commentary on current affairs.'

Owen Roe never actually got to meet PJ Mara. 'I saw him twice, once outside the Shelbourne Hotel and once outside Leinster House. Both times he had his right-hand outstretched to greet people. But I resisted the temptation to walk up and introduce myself!'

In Dermot Morgan's view, Charles Haughey ran out of political rope in the end.

'He was just not equipped to introduce a liberal agenda. His handling of the divorce and abortion referenda seemed very opportunistic. He just ran out of time with the sea change that saw Mary Robinson come into the Park.'

The series had pushed out new frontiers, and sailed close to the wind. There was, in fact, just one threat of a libel action, from Senator Donie Cassidy over a sketch on false hair. But it was never pursued.

The series ended in 1991 and Saturday mornings returned to normal.

Haughey: Mara. Old faithful Mara. Sit down. I have something to say and I want you to be the first to know. As we bid adieu to 1991, another, more painful farewell must be made.

Mara: Yes, Boss.

H: The issue of resignation can no longer be postponed.

M: Yes, Boss.

H: There have been too many scandals, too many budget overruns, too much fiscal ineptitude, public pay unrest.

M: Yes, Boss.

H: No man can go on forever.

M: Yes, Boss.

H: The buck has to stop somewhere.

M: With the man at the top.

H: Or thereabouts, yes.

H: Don't be upset, friend. We have had a good run of it. You were an excellent Sancho Panza to my Don Quixote. We tilted a few windmills, had a few laughs, a few smiles.

M: And an Arms Trial!

H: We had good times, but now we lie slumped in the polls. We face disaster were we to face the electorate now. This is the time. As Hamlet said: 'Now might I do it, pat...'

M: Patrick Joseph, Boss.

H: Shakespeare. The bard. Far better thing I do now, than I ever did before. A resignation is the only thing that will serve the party rank and file now.

M: Yes, Boss.

H: So write yours and I'll give it to them!

M: But.... Boss....!!

H: Maaara!

Evening Herald

19

Papandreou, My Hero

'I care about him, yeah. You can't be that long involved with someone, without caring about them.'

When PJ Mara joined the Fianna Fail Press Office in 1983, he made three promises: One – never to get bored; two – never to drive when drunk, and three – never to get caught in a traffic jam.

He fulfilled promises two and three by travelling almost exclusively by taxi to and from from his Clontarf home.

As Government Press Secretary, he enjoyed the lifestyle that went with the job.

'If PJ had to go to Howth from Clontarf, he would not go by bus!' says the present Press Secretary, Sean Duignan.

The taxi arrived at 8.15am every morning, PJ sat in the back and few words were exchanged during the twenty minute trip to Government buildings.

In fact things were so silent on these trips that on one occasion, the taxi was travelling up Westland Row before the driver realised he had no PJ!

He had heard the back door bang and assumed his passenger was safely on board. However, PJ had been about to get into the vehicle when he realised he had forgotten something. He put in his brief case, shut the door and went back into the house. On emerging less than a minute later, he found his taxi – along with his all-important brief case – had departed, leaving him stranded on Seafield Avenue!

PJ's third promise – never to get bored – was relatively easy to keep when you worked for Charles Haughey. Never far from controversy,

Haughey attracted constant interest both inside and outside Leinster House. A figure either loved or hated by people, there was scarcely any room for middle-ground opinion. His very presence in the Dail Chamber raised the temperature level. When he entered a room, the tension rose immediately and remained so until he decided to leave again.

Life close to this vibrant political figure was always exciting. Defending Haughey against the constant barrage of media allegations required an unusual high level of diplomatic skills.

The tasks Mara was asked to perform often strayed far from the strict role of the media adviser.

The year 1989 saw Haughey, Mara and a group of senior Civil Servants in Athens for the Heads of State meeting during the Greek Presidency of the EC.

Haughey was being briefed by senior aides when much commotion was heard outside.

'What's all the fuss about PJ?' demanded Haughey.

PJ went to the window and looked down.

'It's the Greek Prime Minister, Papandreou arriving at the Press Centre with his young girlfriend, Taoiseach,' reported Mara. (Papandreou's decision to leave his wife for a very young and attractive former air hostess had caused major comment throughout the Community).

'Oh, what's she like – tell me exactly how she looks,' said a totally engrossed Haughey.

Mara departed downstairs to the Press Centre for a better view of the woman. He was back within ten minutes.

'Well, Taoiseach, she's an extremely attractive woman, beautiful in fact. She had every hack in Rhodes drooling.'

Haughey listened to every word with interest, took a deep breath, and softly declared: 'Papandreou, my hero!'

Haughey was always interesting to work with, every turn saw a new and unexpected development.

So what was the relationship between the two men?

Asked in a *Sunday Tribune* interview if he cared about Haughey, Mara replied: 'I care about him, yeah. You can't be that long involved with someone, without caring about them.'

The answer was a major understatement. Mara had given a major portion of his life to looking after Haughey, often without much thanks.

Michael McDowell reckons that in Mara, Haughey recognised someone who was willing to fight with him through the chicken and chips circuit, and who was prepared to get up and get going.

'Charlie needed someone bright and affable, who would offset the GUBU factor. It was not a slave/master relationship, but PJ knew who the paymaster was. He devoted himself assiduously to his job. Charlie's interest was his interest. Charlie saw that he was clever and could be a very valuable part of the team.'

McDowell agrees with most observers that Haughey did not take Mara, nor anybody else, completely into his confidence.

One of Haughey's great capacities was to keep people at a distance. In or out of office, Haughey kept a lot of elbow room around him.

But Mara's complete loyalty amazed many, including journalist Emily O'Reilly.

'I could never understand how, on the one hand he could almost debase himself, and be a complete professional on the other. I can't understand how you would spend so much of your life ensuring that another person's image was up to scratch.'

But there are two sides to every relationship, and Mara did stand to make huge gains.

Emily continues: 'Haughey enabled PJ's social ambitions to be realised in a way which he otherwise could not. He flew on the Government jet, he stayed in the same five star hotels as the Taoiseach. He attended ritzy dos. In a way, PJ also tried to mimic

Haughey's life-style. Nothing but the best. Always the Horse Shoe bar and champagne all the way. He tried to put on the image of being a bit of a rogue like Charlie, but he wasn't.'

PJ disagrees: 'Sometimes Emily seems to misunderstand completely what motivated those of us who were involved in politics with Charles Haughey. The main motivation for all of us was an opportunity to participate in politics at the highest level, to be involved in doing things and achieving things with CJH and he certainly provided all of us with an opportunity to do that. Long hours, hard grinding, a commitment to the task in hand, and, taking our example from him, little interest or attention was paid to the trappings. Indeed he actively discouraged any fascination with such trappings.

'One of the things Emily O'Reilly forgets,' says Mara 'is that hauling your ass around Europe in a government jet and staying in five star hotels becomes very tedious and boring after a short while. As for life-style, the Horse Shoe bar, so-called ritzy dos, champagne and all that crack – I had been there, done that, in my early twenties, long before I every got involved in serious politics.'

Haughey's treatment of Mara was very often not very polite, and he was pushed around like some 'gofor'.

Emily O'Reilly was working in New York in 1984 when Haughey arrived on a fund-raising mission. He was invited to go on a radio show and O'Reilly went along to record the event.

Emily stepped into the back of the large limousine which the radio station sent for him. She was followed by Haughey. Mara proceeded to get in and was about to sit on the jump seat when Haughey's leg shot out:

'Get into the front there, Mara!' he snapped, before proceeding to tell her in great detail of how his favourite drink was a 'bullshot' – a well known cure for a bad hangover!

'To a certain extent O'Reilly is right,' says Mara. 'Haughey could behave in the most appalling fashion at times. But for the most part he was a model of civility. Those of us who worked for him ignored his more extreme outbursts. As a matter of interest, those of use who worked closely with CJH used to collect and savour his more extraordinary outbursts and would amuse each other at regular intervals retelling them to each other when we had a suitably appreciative audience gathered.'

As far as Emily O'Reilly is concerned, Mara was never a close family friend. 'It's interesting', she notes, 'that he never went to any of the Haughey family weddings, whereas "business friends" such as Dermot Desmond did.'

'From 1970 until 1983 Breda and myself were close personal friends with Charles and Maureen Haughey and their family,' says PJ. 'In 1983, when I started to work with Charlie Haughey full-time I had to make a decision, because the nature of the work was so demanding, to have far less social contact with CJH than I had had in the previous thirteen years.'

'It had to be this way to preserve our working relationship because we could not have continued to live in each other's ears 24 hours a day!'

Journalist Sam Smyth sees the relationship in many ways, as close to the caricature in the *Scrap Saturday* series. 'But they were obviously good friends as well. The more Haughey was in government, the more distant they became. Mara was never a confidant.'

Dick Walsh of the *Irish Times*, a long-time Haughey critic, claims the two were attracted by their north-side origins.

'They had a fellow-feeling of being north-siders and Dublin guys. In a way, both were outsiders in Fianna Fail.'

But Mara was, in many ways for Walsh, the more polished of the two, even down to the use of very colourful language.

'Haughey used extraordinary language in private,' says Walsh. 'I have never heard anyone in politics use language like his. PJ probably didn't like it, but he was much more colourful in a different way. Mara was very clever with words.'

This cleverness was frequently used even against certain gossip columnists, whom Mara described as the 'clitorati' – people who wrote about the glitterati!

Walsh condemns the former Taoiseach for not paying enough heed to Mara. 'While he was dependent on PJ, he did not listen to him often enough. He is a very bright individual and he could see what was going on, the decline in support at various times, or the opportunity for headway. He could say these things to Haughey in private, but it would appear that CJH did not take a blind bit of notice of him.'

His influence with Haughey was, in reality, probably quite limited.

As an example, Michael McDowell points to Haughey's attempt to block Michael Mills from being re-appointed Ombudsman in order to settle an old grudge. The PDs intervened and rescued the situation.

'PJ would have known that Haughey was sailing on to a bit of a reef and that there was nothing to be gained by getting rid of Mills. However, I don't think he as much as lifted a finger to stop it.'

But it was Mara's ability to do the job that impressed most people.

'The only time I began to take politics seriously was when I saw PJ didn't,' says Sam Smyth.

A profile of Mara by John Waters in the *Irish Times* in November 1991 said Mara doesn't so much 'do a job, as weave a spell'. Waters continued:

'His social skills are described in terms approaching awe, by even those journalists who know that his job is to pull the wool over their eyes. His *modus operandi* is inseparable from his personality. He creates a web of *bonhomie* and 'laddishness' around himself, which is difficult to resist.

'He has an eye for an individual's weakness and enjoys a capacity to create verbal caricatures which can devastatingly deflate even the most serious of threats to the position of his employer.

'Political journalists speak of his uncanny ability to coin nicknames which focus on the essence of the individual being targetted: a female reporter is known as 'Blonde Ambition,' a diminutive opposition deputy as 'The Jockey', and so on.'

These coinages, although almost always unprintable, spread through the political undergrowth like napalm.

His role as Government Press Secretary will go down in history for its uniqueness.

The current Government Press Secretary, Sean Duignan, stresses that the incumbent of the job is 'simply what the Taoiseach of the day decides he is.'

'The one golden rule is not to be caught out telling lies. But,' adds Duignan, 'the job does not mean you have to deliver stories to journalists all the time.'

Dick Walsh saw Mara's role as a propagandist.

'As a professional he was very good, but as to whether he was someone who could stand aside and see what was going on in an objective way, I would not even bother to ask the question!'

Apart from the newspapers, Mara's other main interest was in RTE and, in particular, in the impact of television.

In this role he had almost daily contact with the editors of current affairs programmes such as *Today Tonight*.

Former editor of the programme, Eugene Murray, recalls a frequently boisterous, but manageable PJ Mara.

'If the Government was totally happy with what you were doing, then you were doing a bad job,' says Murray.

'I had a good working relationship with PJ, but it did boil over from time to time.

'There were mornings I went into the office and had to hold the phone several feet away. I would then say "Thank you PJ", and put the phone down. I would know he had been in with Haughey and had got a grilling!'

During these heated exchanges on the telephone, Mara frequently threatened all sorts of awful happenings on RTE, but never carried them out. Murray pays tribute to Mara for never going over his head, to make a complaint to the station's director general or chairman. Both former Fine Gael leader, Alan Dukes, and the Press Officer of the Labour party, Fergus Finlay, did.

'In many ways,' says Eamon Dunphy, 'PJ was a victim of his own good nature. He probably got a much higher profile than CJH wanted. But he served him magnificently, he took a lot of poison out of people like me. I said to myself: "If he's employing PJ, then Haughey can't really be that bad!"'

20

PJ Gets his Wings

'I firmly believe there is a life outside of politics.'

Asked by a reporter in December 1991, if he could afford to put his feet up when he retired, PJ Mara replied that he could not.

'Like yourself I spend my salary every month. Like yourself I wait for my next cheque to arrive!'

Although earning an annual salary of almost £50,000 per annum, PJ Mara was not a man to store up spare cash. He and Breda had seen some good times, and some very lean ones. But there was always enough to get by.

For almost ten years, PJ Mara had worked night and day for Charles Haughey and Fianna Fail. For almost ten years his wife and son had seen very little of him except during summer holidays and at Christmas. More often than not, Breda and John would be asleep before PJ got home from work, and he would be long gone in the morning before they awoke. Often, the only inter-family communication was hand-written notes which PJ would leave for Breda, and telephone calls during the day.

In August of 1991, PJ took his family to Kinvara as normal. While there, he thought long and hard about his future. Now approaching 50 years of age, he decided it was time for change.

His career move was prompted primarily by the fact that Charles Haughey had been given some indications that he would be stepping down in the not-too-distant future. He was reluctant to let go of the reins of power, however, and it became increasingly clear that another heave was brewing.

'There's only one time to leave power, and that's when you're dragged roaring and screaming,' PJ joked, when he addressed a European journalists' lunch in the Westbury Hotel in Dublin.

So, in the summer of 1991, PJ Mara told his wife that he intended to abandon politics and return to private life.

'I said to her that I intended to become a private soldier again, and go into business to try to make some money!' he recalls.

'I also firmly believed there was a life outside politics. I had discussed this often with people like former Minister John Boland who was very happy to go on and make a career in law.'

Through the grape-vine, PJ let it be known that he was planning a move. He did no more than that, and never lobbied for any job.

But soon the offers arrived, mainly through business contacts. The offers centred around public relations of one kind or another, and organisational skills.

Sharp-eyed business men like Paul McGuinness had long spotted Mara's unique skills.

'PJ always had an excellent career ahead of him,' says Paul McGuinness. 'He looked on politics almost as another branch of showbusiness and so adapted very easily. I, for one, would be delighted to do business with him at any time.'

PJ Mara had, in fact, tentatively accepted a combination of offers when the GPA offer 'came along'.

'The offer from GPA was very interesting and challenging,' he says. 'They were always people I admired, and I was delighted to take it.

'GPA is a magnificent organisation and is staffed by magnificent people. What Tony Ryan and his colleagues have done in GPA is an inspiration and an example to all Irish entrepeneurs. In this country we often talk about how well educated and intelligent our young people are. Tony Ryan and GPA is one of the few organisations in this country that has gathered together hundreds of these extraordinary bright young people and let them loose on the markets of the world. Their achievement is nothing less that stunning, dealing with airline customers in every corner of the globe stretching from the Urals to Tierra del Fuego, doing sophisticated deals in dozens of different cultures and legal jurisdictions and all of this work being managed and directed from Shannon.

'My admiration for what has been achieved by Tony Ryan and GPA is unbounded.'

So, ironically, PJ Mara was to move from his old boss, Charlie Haughey to a company where one of his new bosses would be former Taoiseach, Dr Garret FitzGerald, a prominent member of the Board of GPA. Life had again turned a full circle!

The story of Guinness Peat Aviation had been truly amazing. And it was largely the story of one man, Tony Ryan.

Born and educated in Thurles, his main ambition while at school was to play hurling in the premier colours. But he never succeeded in this ambition.

The son of a train driver, he said in one interview: 'My family has been in the transport business for 1,000 years!'

Ryan joined Aer Lingus as a clerk and 1956 and swiftly moved up through the company.

Addressing the IMI Conference in Killarney in 1991 he described how once, while living in Asia in 1974, 'I stopped to watch a food vendor whom I passed each day. He was a banana-chip maker. His business was to slice, cook and sell bananas to passers-by. He was extraordinarily skilful, not only in slicing hundreds of bananas into thousands of perfect pieces, but also at selling the product. He impressed me and made me think.

'I felt it was a pity that such marketing, technical talent and energy was devoted to a process which sold for a mere penny. There and then I determined that when I went into business on my own account I would apply my energy to developing and marketing a big-ticket product which could sell for vastly more. It could have been property, ships or aircraft.'

Funded with just £50,000 he managed to put GPA together, and began leasing aircraft. The small team of dedicated people around him worked all hours to help it eventually become a dominant force in world aircraft leasing.

By 1991, Ryan had managed to attract some of the top business and political names to the board of his company. These included men like Sir John Harvey-Jones, the former chairman of ICI, Lord Lawson, the former Chancellor of the Exchequer, former Taoiseach Dr Garret FitzGerald, former Secretary of the Department of Foreign Affairs Sean Donlon and former EC Commissioner Peter Sutherland.

GPA and Tony Ryan always kept a low profile. He scarcely ever gave interviews and media queries were answered with the minimal response. Staff were under strict orders not to talk to journalists.

As a private company, GPA had obligations only to its shareholders.

Dr Tony Ryan had always been inherently against his brainchild going public, but reluctantly agreed in 1991 in order to fund a major programme of expansion.

The move meant that certain key executives like Maurice Foley began to become more accessible to the media. But this was not enough. It was decided to appoint a special internal adviser and public relations consultant.

Director Sean Donlon had long known PJ Mara. A regular social contact, he was one of the regular attenders for lunch in the Unicorn on Saturdays.

One Saturday when PJ had just retired as Government Press Secretary, Donlon arrived in the Unicorn with a giant print of nearby hostelry, Doheny and Nesbitts. He passed it around for the regular diners to sign. Among those who signed was Brenda O'Hanlon, PR adviser to Mary Robinson during her presidential campaign.

It fell to PJ Mara's lot to fight off the negative publicity surrounding the upcoming GPA flotation in London and elsewhere.

'Witty and gregarious, Mara was the antithesis of the management types at GPA,' wrote Matt Cooper in the *Sunday Business Post*. 'It was expected that he would be able to endear himself to the most truculent of media people.'

When Mara took up his post with GPA, he thought long and hard about the complex world of financial journalism in the City of London. He had many contacts in London and New York and the various capitals of Europe from his time as Government Press Secretary. He had particular friendships with journalists in the *Financial Times,* the *Sunday Times,* the *Telegraph Group* and Reuters. In the weeks that followed, Mara spent long hours and days working with and briefing these writers. He spent a lot of time in the City of London and in New York, particularly when GPA executives were conducting their roadshows making presentations to the various financial institutions in those cities. It was a tough assignment, but the general feeling is that in the short time available to him, he made a considerable impact, particularly in the UK quality financial press. It is generally accepted that the relationships that he cemented during that short spell and the trust and confidence he engendered will pay considerable dividends in the months and years ahead.

On 19 April, the *Sunday Business Post* published a report that existing institutional shareholders in GPA had not agreed to the condition set down that they should hold onto the vast majority of their shares for at least one year after the flotation. The story was picked up by the British press.

Further detailed analysis caused equal concern. There was worry about the company's policy of aircraft depreciation, and almost near-failure to understand the company's complex funding methods. Observers wondered how GPA could blandly claim it planned to spend $21 billion when the flotation was set to bring in just $650 million.

GPA and PJ Mara mounted a Herculean effort to defend their proposals. Favourable comment came from the *Observer* and the *Sunday Times*. But the highly influential *Financial Times* kept lobbing in the missiles in the days before the flotation.

As journalist Matt Cooper put it: 'Despite all Mara's work, it appeared that some commentators remembered what they considered the arrogant manner in which they had been treated in the old days. GPA had become nice too late.'

A final blow was struck when the London Stock Exchange refused GPA a place on the FTSE 100, the share index guide to Britain's top companies. In February of 1992, GPA, along with two other Irish companies, AIB (under the chairmanship of Peter Sutherland) and the Smurfit Group made a joint application, but it was turned down.

The road-shows continued with financial advisers Goldman Sachs even venturing to suggest an increase in the proposed number of shares.

But the alarm bells soon started to ring.

On Tuesday, 16 June the day before the expected flotation, Ryan was forced to cancel a Bloomsday breakfast with his old friend, architect Sam Stephenson in the Cafe Royale in London.

Finally, on Wednesday morning, a meeting of the Board attended by among others, Garret FitzGerald and Lord Lawson, agreed that the flotation would have to be cancelled.

Goldman Sachs were apportioned much of the blame. It was pointed out that Davy Stockbrokers in Dublin managed to sell more shares than they did in the whole of the United States!

But, according to one institutional fund manager, it was GPA's senior management's stubbornness on the share price that sealed their fate. The company management's own personal wealth was too tied up in the share price, he claimed.

The complex reasons for GPA's failure to take off was explained very simply by James Halstead of London Stockbrokers, Hoare

Govett: 'What happened to GPA was the same as a person trying to buy a house, finding out that the bank did not want to lend 90 per cent of the purchase price.'

And what of PJ Mara's role in all of this?

Like all other staff, Mara is reluctant to talk about GPA, or why the flotation collapsed.

'Mara was drafted in at far too short notice,' says *Irish Press* financial journalist, Pat Boyle. 'When they were undertaking a venture of this kind, their man should have been in place long before he was.'

According to observers, the company was often found floundering and unable to cope with the statements made in the *Financial Times*. While Mara had many of the Irish and British journalists 'eating out of his hand' – all were anxious to get a look inside the inner sanctum of GPA headquarters in Shannon – the tougher analysts had made their minds up.

But the collapse may ironically extend PJ Mara's period of employment at GPA. While he refuses to comment on the terms of his contract, it's understood it is for one year on a salary of £100,000 in addition to generous expenses. All GPA staff, for example, fly exclusively first class and stay only in five star hotels.

GPA is likely to go public at some future date. Observers put that date at least two years down the road. In the meantime, PJ Mara can expect to fill a useful and more important role as he comes to grips with the bizarre world of high finance.

The job is ideally suited to his new life-style. Having spent the weekend at his new country home in his beloved Kinvara, he can set out each Monday morning for the 8am meeting in Shannon headquarters.

Later in the week he may transfer to the equally opulent and comfortable surroundings of the company's Dublin office, at 26 Upper Pembroke St. The office is only a short walking distance from the Mara's new city home on the very fashionable Wellington Road. His old haunt of yesteryear, the Horse Shoe bar is but a stone's throw!

21

Reflections

'I had a very good time.'

PJ Mara spent August of 1991 on holiday in Co. Galway. As usual, he spent his normal four weeks' summer leave with his wife Breda, and son John, taking a break from the day-to-day happenings in Government Buildings.

While in the Burren, however, he planned out a lot of serious work on the administrative side of his job as Government Press Secretary.

'I made a lot of notes and committed a lot of thoughts to paper during that holiday. I had them all neatly typed up in a file on my return to Dublin,' he recalls.

Six months later the file remained unopened on PJ Mara's desk.

His last period in office was to be absorbed in 'fire-fighting tactics,' dealing with the constant stream of barrage and abuse that originated with the Greencore controversy, the story which first broke on Sunday, 1 September, the day he returned from his holidays.

'I was aware of the Greencore story because I had met journalist Sam Smyth when I returned to Dublin for a couple of days in mid-August to attend to some family business. I felt it wasn't something that particularly concerned me, because neither the Government nor Fianna Fail had any connection with the individuals involved.

'How wrong I was. The Greencore affair was to become the first of a series of events that de-stabilised the last administration of Charles Haughey.'

The last days were difficult for everybody in Government Buildings.

'During that time CJH was subjected to a barrage of abuse, vilification and insult, that sometimes was just beyond belief. It was, as I said before, like Alice on a night out with Franz Kafka in Wonderland. But the Taoiseach behaved in an incredibly dignified way, trying all the time to get on with the business of Government. It was a super-human task.

'Some of the abuse that CJH took during that period from certain commentators was mind-boggling. Week after week, for example, Dr Cruise O'Brien in his various weekly columns maintained a campaign of abuse and vituperation.

'Dr Cruise O'Brien – now there's a gent! His brazeness is spell-binding. Apologist for the more exotic species of Zionism, for those white supremacist sweethearts in Pretoria and for the wilder spirits of Ulster Unionism, this hero has blathered on now for the best part of two decades about the "dangers" of CJH; how Haughey is a "threat" or "danger" to democracy; free speech, the liberal values and principles that we all cherish and hold dear; how motherhood and a Dublin man's affection for his granny would be made Offenses Against the State Act if Charlie Haughey ever got an overall majority.

'Raving on about cloves of garlic, stakes through the heart at the cross-roads at midnight, is it any wonder the decent people of Dublin North-East gave him the gate 15 years ago in the general election of 1977?

'Contrast Dr O'Brien's meanderings about Haughey with the grace that Haughey always showed when he lost office or suffered a defeat. Contrast the sheer daftness of Dr O'Brien's prophecies with the style and manner of Charlie Haughey's resignation as Taoiseach earlier this year.

'Contrast all of this fantasy about Charlie Haughey which poured from Dr O'Brien's pen with the genuinely liberal sentiments expressed by Charles Haughey in a speech to Aosdana in the Royal Hospital, Kilmainham on 14 November 1990, sentiments which he implemented and lived by in Government.

'...Art is, among other things a means to self-recognition and self-knowledge, not only for the artistic but for society as well. It is the burnished mirror in which we recognise ourselves, individually and collectively, as men and women of a particular era and as a nation at a particular stage in its history. In Ireland, in recent years, there has been a great thirst for this sort of self-recognition and an appreciation of those who make it possible.'

Despite the upheavels this was the period during which the Programme for Economic and Social Progress (PESP) was finalised and the second Programme for Government was agreed with the Progressive Democrats. The work of the Anglo-Irish Conference went ahead and the difficult preparations for the European Council at Maastricht were developed and perfected.

Charles Haughey did not talk much about the scandals erupting all around him.

'CJH had an amazing capacity for work and an ability to get on with the tasks in hand in a disciplined and orderly way,' recalls PJ. 'He had no time for histrionics, or sighing about things. Whatever the circumstances, he just got on with the job with full-blooded commitment. And he expected the same commitment from everybody around him.'

Looking back, Mara still regrets that parliamentary questions on these issues were not answered more fully. Such an approach would have allayed the fears of the general public at an early stage, he argues.

When Sean Doherty gave his press conference, Charles Haughey saw his own version of events was no longer believed and he decided to resign.

'Once he decided on a particular course, that was that. There was no great sentimentality on his part. CJH was an absolute realist. He knew and accepted that his race was run.'

Charles Haughey did not cry leaving office. True to his nature, he left with the minimum of fuss and drama. While the new Taoiseach went to Aras An Uachtarain to receive his seal of office, his predecessor walked back across the tunnel to Government Buildings for the last time.

There he spoke and shook hands individually with each member of his personal staff. Many were in tears. Shortly after 12 noon, he emerged from his office at the end of the corridor on the first floor of Government Buildings accompanied by PJ Mara, Martin Mansergh, private secretary Donagh Morgan and personal assistant Catherine Butler. All walked with him to his new temporary office in Leinster House. The era of Charles Haughey as Head of Government had formally ended.

●●●●●●●●●

For PJ Mara, Charles Haughey is the outstanding politician of his generation.

'He will,' says Mara, 'probably go down in history among the three most influential figures of the last half-century,' the other two in his view being Eamon De Valera and Sean Lemass.

'Some of his major achievements, when they are examined by historians, will be the periods he spent as Minister for Justice and Minister for Finance. He will be remembered as a particularly caring politician for the position of the elderly in our society. They, in turn, had a great regard for him, as was evident in the affection shown to him by the elderly on his many trips around the country.

'His whole life was devoted to achieving things, even small key measures. He wasn't one who indulged in any blather. But he consistently wanted things to move along, a little bit each day. He had a wonderful instinct for what the Irish people would accept in the way of change or innovation at any particular time. This instinct sometimes made him appear a bit more cautious than he really was, but he believed that there was no point in bringing forward policies which would not have the support of the people. He had no time for empty gestures or meaningless talk.

'He will also be remembered for his efforts to improve the lot of women. In this regard he set up both the first and second Commissions for the Status of Women, and showed remarkable sensitivity and far-sightedness in his appointments of women to high office, such as Maire Geoghegan-Quinn to the Cabinet (the first woman since Countess Markievicz), and Mella Carroll to the High Court. He was constantly seeking opportunities to promote women to positions of responsibility and power in all areas of public affairs. All of the appointments he made were implemented quietly and effectively in an undramatic way. Examples of this were the number of key appointments of women to the Boards of State companies and organisations in recent times.'

Mara believes that Haughey's early years as Taoiseach are often misunderstood. In the early 1980s he did not have the benefit of a totally united and supportive Government. Many of his colleagues in those earlier Governments were not as committed and supportive of him as they should have been. This, he believes, gave rise to insecurity and apparent indecision in Government.

'The contrast between those early Governments and the Government of 1987 is a stark one. In 1987 Charles Haughey came into Government with a group of totally united and committed colleagues. The public finances were in total disarray. That Government proceeded immediately to deal with the problems of the public finances in an ordered and disciplined fashion. Many of the measures that had to be taken at that time were not likely to be the most popular. That did not matter. The correct decisions were taken for the country's good and any political consequences were ignored.

'Many commentators at that time, Irish as well as British, remained suspicious about how Charles Haughey would behave in Government. They feared that his would be a spendthrift Government, that the

Anglo-Irish Agreement would be ditched and that he would not be able to work closely with the EC Commission. All of these fears were totally misplaced. For years, particularly during his period in Opposition, Charles Haughey had been a firm believer in the economic discipline which the country needed and which the Government of Garret FitzGerald and Dick Spring had shied away from.

'It was very clear to anyone who had been involved in the preparations undertaken by Fianna Fail for a return to Government during their years in Opposition from 1983 to 1987 that this was the case. Even before he had been elected as Taoiseach by the Dail in March 1987, Charles Haughey travelled to Brussels to meet the EC Commission President, Jacques Delors. This was an important meeting at which Delors, then at the height of his powers, promised the Taoiseach designate that he would make all of the Commission's resources available to him in order to resolve the problems of the public finances.

'In particular, Delors offered guidance on debt management, and the need to stabilise the level of the Exchequer borrowing, the twin problems inherited by Haughey from the FitzGerald/Spring Government.

'Out of this little-known initiative emerged the singular role of the EC Commission in Irish national planning. This meeting also sowed the seed for the creation of the National Debt Management Agency under Dr Michael Somers. This initiative is as invaluable to the Reynolds Administration in the present climate as it was to Haughey.

'Later, his negotiation of the PNR and the PESP will be seen as fundamental pillars of the Haughey legacy. During Garret Fitzgerald's and Dick Spring's term in office, all the social partners were deliberately excluded from any participation. More than anything else, this negotiation was his outstanding achievement.

'There is also his track record on the Anglo-Irish Agreement, and the intelligent way he dealt with the British. A lot of people quite illegitimately portrayed him as a bogey-man, a guy who was some kind of closet Provo, a Provo in good tailoring. These were just some of the images. It was a deliberate falsehood designed to smear, purveyed by lesser politicians to knock him.

'Haughey could also be extraordinarily generous to his political opponents, a quality rarely reciprocated. In March 1987, CJH, as incoming Taoiseach took up an invitation from the then US President Ronald Reagan to visit the White House on St Patrick's Day. This was an important and prestigious occasion for an incoming Taoiseach. The outgoing Taoiseach, Dr Garret FitzGerald had his own arrangements made and was going to be in Washington during the same period. Charlie Haughey insisted that Dr FitzGerald attend at all the public functions and occasions that had been arranged for him. It was a remarkably kind gesture by CJH. During that visit Haughey signalled at a luncheon given by the Speaker of the House of Representatives, Jim Wright, his intention to work fully the Anglo-Irish Agreement.'

Mara was impressed by Haughey's deep respect for the institutions of the State.

'It always intrigued me how CJH was so careful in ensuring that correct procedures were adopted and observed in the most meticulous manner in the transaction of public or official business. All the 'i's' dotted, and the 't's' crossed!

'He was never late for any public or official engagement. He was regularly in the Dail Chamber with his Ministers before the Opposition came in. He never kept people waiting. He was an absolute demon for punctuality and would not tolerate anybody being late. He regarded being late for appointments as the height of bad manners and ignorance.'

Mara also singles out Haughey's respect for the Fianna Fail organisation, the party's National Executive and, in particular, the Fianna Fail parliamentary party.

'He was the outstanding parliamentarian of his generation. He knew, understood and loved the Dail like no other politician of his time.

'One of the most interesting things about Haughey is how the people of his own part of the city responded to him. The north side of Dublin is primarily a lower income area, ordinary people working hard to bring up their families and to rear and educate them the best way they can. These were the people, who, over a period of 35 years, consistently gave Haughey comfortable majorities election after election. These real people knew him and trusted him, and voted accordingly.

'As recently as the 1991 local elections, Fianna Fail got almost 50 per cent of the seats in an area stretching from Finglas through Cabra to Clontarf. In the 1989 general election, of the 17 seats on offer on the north side, Fianna Fail under Haughey won 10. There was not one Labour seat, just two for the Workers Party and Fine Gael was reduced to political impotence! All this at a time when the Fianna Fail party was not riding very high in the opinion polls. This real performance speaks louder than any opinion poll.'

Haughey's consistent popularity, despite a generally unfavourable press has made PJ Mara sceptical about the influence of the media. He refers to an example given by Proinsias Mac Aonghusa at one particular conference a number of years ago.

'At that Conference Proinsias pointed out that in both Galway East and West the most important paper right through the 1930s, '40s and '50s was the *Connaught Tribune*. It was the only paper that went into many homes at that time. During that period the *Connaught Tribune* was a unreconstructed Cumann Na nGael/Fine Gael/ Blueshirt paper, and always took a FG line at election time. But yet the people of Galway East and West always returned overwhelming Fianna Fail majorities! There is a certain lesson in that. Politicians can get too concerned with what appears in papers.

'Since I left politics, I read the political coverage less carefully than I used to, but I suspect I'm still reading it more carefully than most people not involved in politics (old habits die hard!). Politicians over-estimate the influence of the press in their affairs.'

PJ Mara may no longer be part of Leinster House, but he still maintains contact with his friends there, many of them ex-members or members of the Cabinet. He has always enjoyed a particular friend-ship with Ray Burke.

'I regard Ray as one of the few people dismissed by Albert Reynolds who has any real political future. He was an outstanding Minister for Justice. When he was removed from office, he was just coming into his own and beginning to show what he really was capable of as a major politician. Burke has one quality which is essential in politics –he can sense danger before it appears over the horizon. He has terrific politi-cal antennae, and has an enormous, natural intelligence. He always had the ability to reduce every political situation to its bare essentials. He has a considerable future ahead of him because he is young enough to recover, once the political climate settles down.'

Mara has a lot of admiration for some of the new members of Government.

'Charlie McCreevy and I have been close friends for a long time. We had a lot of fun together and we share many of the same attitudes. I suspect that when he gets some experience in Cabinet behind him, he will be a formidable member of future governments, and a serious force in coming times.

'Brian Cowen, though much younger, is a formidable debater. He has a clear mind and is an excellent communicator. He also comes from a terrific Fianna Fail party background in Laois/Offaly, an area I regard as the party heartland in rural Ireland. We will see and hear a lot more of him in the years ahead.

'Michael Smith is a quiet, effective performer in Government. I had a lot of dealings with him and regard him as one of the most serious ministers in the present Government. He gets his work done in a quiet way without any attention-seeking, but is all the more effective because of that.

'David Andrews is one of my oldest friends in politics and I'm delighted to see him get his chance on the international stage. He is making a great impression, and, from talking to my media friends in places like London and New York, he is a first-class ambassador for Ireland.

'Bertie Ahern has had a hard time in the first six months of this Government, and unjustly so. A lot of the conventional wisdom knocking about at the moment claims that Bertie is in the hands of the Revenue or his Civil Servants. This is bullshit and will be seen to be bullshit in the future. When he took over the job he had to prepare the Estimates and the Budget against a background of further demands by the PDs for tax cuts.

'Unfortunately, to achieve this PD demand, some tax breaks had to be attacked and many lost out, particularly those in the corporate sector. The spin that was put on this was that Bertie was not his own man, but purely guided by the Civil Servants. This is not the case. As he gains more experience, Bertie will be an outstanding Minister for Finance.

'Maire Geoghegan-Quinn is a formidable lady who is going to be a dominant figure in our affairs over the coming years, either here at home or in the wider European Community. She has a terrific presence and is a considerable performer in the Dail. She has minor constituency problems, which, if she applied her mind a bit more to it, could be dealt with rather easily. She is, and should be, an inspirational figure for all women who aspire to leadership in politics or public affairs.

'Seamus Brenan is a politician who has achieved a lot for Fianna Fail in the south side of Dublin. He was doing quite will in his communications and transport briefs and I think an Economic posting might suit him better than Education.'

One of the interesting thing about PJ Mara is that through good years and bad, through periods of tranquillity and periods of turmoil he has maintain very good relationships with politicians from opposition groups and indeed, has formed close friendships with many of them. Among those he admires in Fine Gael would be John Boland, and Pat Cooney former minister in the Fine Gael/Labour government of 1983-1987, Senator Maurice Manning and Deputy Brendan McGahan from Co. Louth. Michael McDowell chairman of the Progressive Democrats, the man most people love to hate, is a good friend of Mara's. In the Labour Party the politician PJ thinks is really interesting and outstanding is Michael D. Higgins. PJ is very fond of independent Senators John A. Murphy and Joe O'Toole.

'All of these people', Mara says 'are very strong-minded individuals, good communicators, great company and most important of all, are not boring.' To be boring, to Mara's way of thinking is the only real sin.

One group in our modern Irish society that Mara has no time for is the new right – 'the so called "moral majority", this bunch of self-appointed "lay mullahs",' as he describes them, who have, it seems to him, taken over from ordained priests and Bishops in offering guidance and direction in matters of faith and morals.

In his view, these people are just as unattractive as the budding commissars of the extreme left were in the 1970s. Both groups have one quality in common – they are both bullies. 'The right-wing groups, young or old, who are demanding referendums on abortion should be ignored,' he says. 'They are a phantom army. Albert Reynolds and the government should confront them. Legislators elected by the people should deal with these problems by legislation and if they don't the people will deal with them.'

One of the interesting developments in Irish society that PJ Mara has noticed in recent years is the decline in esteem for politicians.

'When I came into politics all the excitement was in public life. The really interesting figures those days were people like Donough

O'Malley, Paddy Hillery, Neil Blaney, Brian Lenihan and Charlie Haughey. These were the people who were setting the pace and capturing the imaginations of the young people.

'Now all that seems to have changed. We seem to be entering a greyer era in public life and all the excitement is now being created by people in the theatre, in music, in poetry and in general in the arts. Today's heroes are Brian Friel, Noel Pearson, Paul McGuinness, Bono, Jim Sheriden, Tom Murphy, Seamus Heaney, Paul Durcan and Tony Cronin.

The late John Healy was generally regarded as an outstanding journalist. But, in my view he was more than that. He was, in reality, a public figure, and a dominant one at that. His opinions, his views and his prejudices were an important part of what we were. I wish we had someone now writing and working and commenting on public affairs like him.

'In business there are names which capture the imagination nowadays like Tony Ryan, Tony O'Reilly, Pat O'Neill, Craig McKinney, Dermot Desmond and Denis Brosnan. I think it is a great pity that political figures who are answerable to an electorate are not more inspirational.'

●●●●●●●●●

PJ Mara's life has been an interesting medley. Aged 50, he has still a major contribution to make, but it will be a contribution made very much outside the world of politics.

His gracious style and charm will be much missed in the corridors of Leinster House for many a year, as will the figure of his mentor, Charles Haughey.

When the history of twentieth-century Dublin comes to be written, Mara, like Haughey, will be signalled out as an influential figure in both political and social circles.

Those who will pay tribute to him will speak fulsomely of him. His own epitaph is, true to character, a simple one-liner. He summed it all up while chatting with former Century Radio political correspondent, Caroline Erskine in May of 1992:

'I had a very good time!'

Bibliography

Browne, Vincent (ed) *Magill Book of Irish Politics*, Magill, 1981.

Browne, Vincent (ed) *Election '82*, Magill, 1982.

Browne, Vincent (ed) *Election '87*, Magill, 1987.

Collins, Stephen *The Haughey File*, The O'Brien Press, 1992.

Cooney, John *Crozier and the Dail*, Mercier, 1986.

Farrell, Michael (ed) *Magill Book of Irish Politics 1984*, Magill, 1984.

Farrelly, Jim *Who's Who in Irish Politics*, Blackwater Press, 1989.

Kenny, Shane *Go Dance of Somebody Else's Grave*, Kildanore, 1990.

Lenihan, Brian *For the Record*, Blackwater Press, 1991

Murtagh, Peter and Joyce, Joe *The Boss*, Poolbeg, 1983.

O'Mahony, T.P. *Jack Lynch, A Biography*, Blackwater Press, 1991.

O'Reilly, Emily *Candidate*, Attic Press, 1991.